C-2067

THIS IS YOUR **PASSBOOK**® FOR ...

ENVIRONMENTAL CONTROL SPECIALIST TRAINEE

N L C®

NATIONAL LEARNING CORPORATION®

passbooks.com

COPYRIGHT NOTICE

Copyright © 2020 by

National Learning Corporation

212 Michael Drive, Syosset, NY 11791
(516) 921-8888 • www.passbooks.com
E-mail: info@passbooks.com

PUBLISHED IN THE UNITED STATES OF AMERICA

PASSBOOK® SERIES

THE *PASSBOOK® SERIES* has been created to prepare applicants and candidates for the ultimate academic battlefield – the examination room.

At some time in our lives, each and every one of us may be required to take an examination – for validation, matriculation, admission, qualification, registration, certification, or licensure.

Based on the assumption that every applicant or candidate has met the basic formal educational standards, has taken the required number of courses, and read the necessary texts, the *PASSBOOK® SERIES* furnishes the one special preparation which may assure passing with confidence, instead of failing with insecurity. Examination questions – together with answers – are furnished as the basic vehicle for study so that the mysteries of the examination and its compounding difficulties may be eliminated or diminished by a sure method.

This book is meant to help you pass your examination provided that you qualify and are serious in your objective.

The entire field is reviewed through the huge store of content information which is succinctly presented through a provocative and challenging approach – the question-and-answer method.

A climate of success is established by furnishing the correct answers at the end of each test.

You soon learn to recognize types of questions, forms of questions, and patterns of questioning. You may even begin to anticipate expected outcomes.

You perceive that many questions are repeated or adapted so that you can gain acute insights, which may enable you to score many sure points.

You learn how to confront new questions, or types of questions, and to attack them confidently and work out the correct answers.

You note objectives and emphases, and recognize pitfalls and dangers, so that you may make positive educational adjustments.

Moreover, you are kept fully informed in relation to new concepts, methods, practices, and directions in the field.

You discover that you arre actually taking the examination all the time: you are preparing for the examination by "taking" an examination, not by reading extraneous and/or supererogatory textbooks.

In short, this PASSBOOK®, used directedly, should be an important factor in helping you to pass your test.

ENVIRONMENTAL CONTROL SPECIALIST TRAINEE

DUTIES
Under direct supervision, receives training, learns and participates in inspections and investigations to determine the causes, effect, and extent of various types of environmental pollution. Performs related duties as required. This is a competitive class trainee position. The period of trainee services shall be one year from the date of appointment from an appropriate eligible list, the service to be of such designated length as to satisfy the training and experience requirements for Environmental Control Specialist. Upon the satisfactory completion of the designated trainee service, which also serves as the probationary period, Environmental Control Specialist Trainees shall obtain permanent status as Environmental Control Specialist.

SUBJECT OF EXAMINATION
Written test designed to test for knowledge, skills and/or abilities in such areas as:
1. Understanding and interpreting written material;
2. Preparing written material;
3. Understanding and interpreting tabular material;
4. Quantitative reasoning.

HOW TO TAKE A TEST

I. YOU MUST PASS AN EXAMINATION

A. *WHAT EVERY CANDIDATE SHOULD KNOW*

Examination applicants often ask us for help in preparing for the written test. What can I study in advance? What kinds of questions will be asked? How will the test be given? How will the papers be graded?

As an applicant for a civil service examination, you may be wondering about some of these things. Our purpose here is to suggest effective methods of advance study and to describe civil service examinations.

Your chances for success on this examination can be increased if you know how to prepare. Those "pre-examination jitters" can be reduced if you know what to expect. You can even experience an adventure in good citizenship if you know why civil service exams are given.

B. *WHY ARE CIVIL SERVICE EXAMINATIONS GIVEN?*

Civil service examinations are important to you in two ways. As a citizen, you want public jobs filled by employees who know how to do their work. As a job seeker, you want a fair chance to compete for that job on an equal footing with other candidates. The best-known means of accomplishing this two-fold goal is the competitive examination.

Exams are widely publicized throughout the nation. They may be administered for jobs in federal, state, city, municipal, town or village governments or agencies.

Any citizen may apply, with some limitations, such as the age or residence of applicants. Your experience and education may be reviewed to see whether you meet the requirements for the particular examination. When these requirements exist, they are reasonable and applied consistently to all applicants. Thus, a competitive examination may cause you some uneasiness now, but it is your privilege and safeguard.

C. *HOW ARE CIVIL SERVICE EXAMS DEVELOPED?*

Examinations are carefully written by trained technicians who are specialists in the field known as "psychological measurement," in consultation with recognized authorities in the field of work that the test will cover. These experts recommend the subject matter areas or skills to be tested; only those knowledges or skills important to your success on the job are included. The most reliable books and source materials available are used as references. Together, the experts and technicians judge the difficulty level of the questions.

Test technicians know how to phrase questions so that the problem is clearly stated. Their ethics do not permit "trick" or "catch" questions. Questions may have been tried out on sample groups, or subjected to statistical analysis, to determine their usefulness.

Written tests are often used in combination with performance tests, ratings of training and experience, and oral interviews. All of these measures combine to form the best-known means of finding the right person for the right job.

II. HOW TO PASS THE WRITTEN TEST

A. *NATURE OF THE EXAMINATION*

To prepare intelligently for civil service examinations, you should know how they differ from school examinations you have taken. In school you were assigned certain definite pages to read or subjects to cover. The examination questions were quite detailed and usually emphasized memory. Civil service exams, on the other hand, try to discover your present ability to perform the duties of a position, plus your potentiality to learn these duties. In other words, a civil service exam attempts to predict how successful you will be. Questions cover such a broad area that they cannot be as minute and detailed as school exam questions.

In the public service similar kinds of work, or positions, are grouped together in one "class." This process is known as *position-classification*. All the positions in a class are paid according to the salary range for that class. One class title covers all of these positions, and they are all tested by the same examination.

B. *FOUR BASIC STEPS*

1) Study the announcement

How, then, can you know what subjects to study? Our best answer is: "Learn as much as possible about the class of positions for which you've applied." The exam will test the knowledge, skills and abilities needed to do the work.

Your most valuable source of information about the position you want is the official exam announcement. This announcement lists the training and experience qualifications. Check these standards and apply only if you come reasonably close to meeting them.

The brief description of the position in the examination announcement offers some clues to the subjects which will be tested. Think about the job itself. Review the duties in your mind. Can you perform them, or are there some in which you are rusty? Fill in the blank spots in your preparation.

Many jurisdictions preview the written test in the exam announcement by including a section called "Knowledge and Abilities Required," "Scope of the Examination," or some similar heading. Here you will find out specifically what fields will be tested.

2) Review your own background

Once you learn in general what the position is all about, and what you need to know to do the work, ask yourself which subjects you already know fairly well and which need improvement. You may wonder whether to concentrate on improving your strong areas or on building some background in your fields of weakness. When the announcement has specified "some knowledge" or "considerable knowledge," or has used adjectives like "beginning principles of…" or "advanced … methods," you can get a clue as to the number and difficulty of questions to be asked in any given field. More questions, and hence broader coverage, would be included for those subjects which are more important in the work. Now weigh your strengths and weaknesses against the job requirements and prepare accordingly.

3) Determine the level of the position

Another way to tell how intensively you should prepare is to understand the level of the job for which you are applying. Is it the entering level? In other words, is this the position in which beginners in a field of work are hired? Or is it an intermediate or advanced level? Sometimes this is indicated by such words as "Junior" or "Senior" in the class title. Other jurisdictions use Roman numerals to designate the level – Clerk I, Clerk II, for example. The word "Supervisor" sometimes appears in the title. If the level is not indicated by the title, check the description of duties. Will you be working under very close supervision, or will you have responsibility for independent decisions in this work?

4) Choose appropriate study materials

Now that you know the subjects to be examined and the relative amount of each subject to be covered, you can choose suitable study materials. For beginning level jobs, or even advanced ones, if you have a pronounced weakness in some aspect of your training, read a modern, standard textbook in that field. Be sure it is up to date and has general coverage. Such books are normally available at your library, and the librarian will be glad to help you locate one. For entry-level positions, questions of appropriate difficulty are chosen – neither highly advanced questions, nor those too simple. Such questions require careful thought but not advanced training.

If the position for which you are applying is technical or advanced, you will read more advanced, specialized material. If you are already familiar with the basic principles of your field, elementary textbooks would waste your time. Concentrate on advanced textbooks and technical periodicals. Think through the concepts and review difficult problems in your field.

These are all general sources. You can get more ideas on your own initiative, following these leads. For example, training manuals and publications of the government agency which employs workers in your field can be useful, particularly for technical and professional positions. A letter or visit to the government department involved may result in more specific study suggestions, and certainly will provide you with a more definite idea of the exact nature of the position you are seeking.

III. KINDS OF TESTS

Tests are used for purposes other than measuring knowledge and ability to perform specified duties. For some positions, it is equally important to test ability to make adjustments to new situations or to profit from training. In others, basic mental abilities not dependent on information are essential. Questions which test these things may not appear as pertinent to the duties of the position as those which test for knowledge and information. Yet they are often highly important parts of a fair examination. For very general questions, it is almost impossible to help you direct your study efforts. What we can do is to point out some of the more common of these general abilities needed in public service positions and describe some typical questions.

1) General information

Broad, general information has been found useful for predicting job success in some kinds of work. This is tested in a variety of ways, from vocabulary lists to questions about current events. Basic background in some field of work, such as sociology or economics, may be sampled in a group of questions. Often these are principles which have become familiar to most persons through exposure rather than through formal training. It is difficult to advise you how to study for these questions; being alert to the world around you is our best suggestion.

2) Verbal ability

An example of an ability needed in many positions is verbal or language ability. Verbal ability is, in brief, the ability to use and understand words. Vocabulary and grammar tests are typical measures of this ability. Reading comprehension or paragraph interpretation questions are common in many kinds of civil service tests. You are given a paragraph of written material and asked to find its central meaning.

3) Numerical ability

Number skills can be tested by the familiar arithmetic problem, by checking paired lists of numbers to see which are alike and which are different, or by interpreting charts and graphs. In the latter test, a graph may be printed in the test booklet which you are asked to use as the basis for answering questions.

4) Observation

A popular test for law-enforcement positions is the observation test. A picture is shown to you for several minutes, then taken away. Questions about the picture test your ability to observe both details and larger elements.

5) Following directions

In many positions in the public service, the employee must be able to carry out written instructions dependably and accurately. You may be given a chart with several columns, each column listing a variety of information. The questions require you to carry out directions involving the information given in the chart.

6) Skills and aptitudes

Performance tests effectively measure some manual skills and aptitudes. When the skill is one in which you are trained, such as typing or shorthand, you can practice. These tests are often very much like those given in business school or high school courses. For many of the other skills and aptitudes, however, no short-time preparation can be made. Skills and abilities natural to you or that you have developed throughout your lifetime are being tested.

Many of the general questions just described provide all the data needed to answer the questions and ask you to use your reasoning ability to find the answers. Your best preparation for these tests, as well as for tests of facts and ideas, is to be at your physical and mental best. You, no doubt, have your own methods of getting into an exam-taking mood and keeping "in shape." The next section lists some ideas on this subject.

IV. KINDS OF QUESTIONS

Only rarely is the "essay" question, which you answer in narrative form, used in civil service tests. Civil service tests are usually of the short-answer type. Full instructions for answering these questions will be given to you at the examination. But in case this is your first experience with short-answer questions and separate answer sheets, here is what you need to know:

1) Multiple-choice Questions

Most popular of the short-answer questions is the "multiple choice" or "best answer" question. It can be used, for example, to test for factual knowledge, ability to solve problems or judgment in meeting situations found at work.

A multiple-choice question is normally one of three types—

- It can begin with an incomplete statement followed by several possible endings. You are to find the one ending which *best* completes the statement, although some of the others may not be entirely wrong.
- It can also be a complete statement in the form of a question which is answered by choosing one of the statements listed.
- It can be in the form of a problem – again you select the best answer.

Here is an example of a multiple-choice question with a discussion which should give you some clues as to the method for choosing the right answer:

When an employee has a complaint about his assignment, the action which will *best* help him overcome his difficulty is to
   A. discuss his difficulty with his coworkers
   B. take the problem to the head of the organization
   C. take the problem to the person who gave him the assignment
   D. say nothing to anyone about his complaint

In answering this question, you should study each of the choices to find which is best. Consider choice "A" – Certainly an employee may discuss his complaint with fellow employees, but no change or improvement can result, and the complaint remains unresolved. Choice "B" is a poor choice since the head of the organization probably does not know what assignment you have been given, and taking your problem to him is known as "going over the head" of the supervisor. The supervisor, or person who made the assignment, is the person who can clarify it or correct any injustice. Choice "C" is, therefore, correct. To say nothing, as in choice "D," is unwise. Supervisors have and interest in knowing the problems employees are facing, and the employee is seeking a solution to his problem.

2) True/False Questions

The "true/false" or "right/wrong" form of question is sometimes used. Here a complete statement is given. Your job is to decide whether the statement is right or wrong.

SAMPLE: A roaming cell-phone call to a nearby city costs less than a non-roaming call to a distant city.

This statement is wrong, or false, since roaming calls are more expensive.
This is not a complete list of all possible question forms, although most of the others are variations of these common types. You will always get complete directions for

answering questions. Be sure you understand *how* to mark your answers – ask questions until you do.

V. RECORDING YOUR ANSWERS

Computer terminals are used more and more today for many different kinds of exams.

For an examination with very few applicants, you may be told to record your answers in the test booklet itself. Separate answer sheets are much more common. If this separate answer sheet is to be scored by machine – and this is often the case – it is highly important that you mark your answers correctly in order to get credit.

An electronic scoring machine is often used in civil service offices because of the speed with which papers can be scored. Machine-scored answer sheets must be marked with a pencil, which will be given to you. This pencil has a high graphite content which responds to the electronic scoring machine. As a matter of fact, stray dots may register as answers, so do not let your pencil rest on the answer sheet while you are pondering the correct answer. Also, if your pencil lead breaks or is otherwise defective, ask for another.

Since the answer sheet will be dropped in a slot in the scoring machine, be careful not to bend the corners or get the paper crumpled.

The answer sheet normally has five vertical columns of numbers, with 30 numbers to a column. These numbers correspond to the question numbers in your test booklet. After each number, going across the page are four or five pairs of dotted lines. These short dotted lines have small letters or numbers above them. The first two pairs may also have a "T" or "F" above the letters. This indicates that the first two pairs only are to be used if the questions are of the true-false type. If the questions are multiple choice, disregard the "T" and "F" and pay attention only to the small letters or numbers.

Answer your questions in the manner of the sample that follows:

32. The largest city in the United States is
    A. Washington, D.C.
    B. New York City
    C. Chicago
    D. Detroit
    E. San Francisco

1) Choose the answer you think is best. (New York City is the largest, so "B" is correct.)
2) Find the row of dotted lines numbered the same as the question you are answering. (Find row number 32)
3) Find the pair of dotted lines corresponding to the answer. (Find the pair of lines under the mark "B.")
4) Make a solid black mark between the dotted lines.

VI. BEFORE THE TEST

Common sense will help you find procedures to follow to get ready for an examination. Too many of us, however, overlook these sensible measures. Indeed, nervousness and fatigue have been found to be the most serious reasons why applicants fail to do their best on civil service tests. Here is a list of reminders:

- Begin your preparation early – Don't wait until the last minute to go scurrying around for books and materials or to find out what the position is all about.
- Prepare continuously – An hour a night for a week is better than an all-night cram session. This has been definitely established. What is more, a night a week for a month will return better dividends than crowding your study into a shorter period of time.
- Locate the place of the exam – You have been sent a notice telling you when and where to report for the examination. If the location is in a different town or otherwise unfamiliar to you, it would be well to inquire the best route and learn something about the building.
- Relax the night before the test – Allow your mind to rest. Do not study at all that night. Plan some mild recreation or diversion; then go to bed early and get a good night's sleep.
- Get up early enough to make a leisurely trip to the place for the test – This way unforeseen events, traffic snarls, unfamiliar buildings, etc. will not upset you.
- Dress comfortably – A written test is not a fashion show. You will be known by number and not by name, so wear something comfortable.
- Leave excess paraphernalia at home – Shopping bags and odd bundles will get in your way. You need bring only the items mentioned in the official notice you received; usually everything you need is provided. Do not bring reference books to the exam. They will only confuse those last minutes and be taken away from you when in the test room.
- Arrive somewhat ahead of time – If because of transportation schedules you must get there very early, bring a newspaper or magazine to take your mind off yourself while waiting.
- Locate the examination room – When you have found the proper room, you will be directed to the seat or part of the room where you will sit. Sometimes you are given a sheet of instructions to read while you are waiting. Do not fill out any forms until you are told to do so; just read them and be prepared.
- Relax and prepare to listen to the instructions
- If you have any physical problem that may keep you from doing your best, be sure to tell the test administrator. If you are sick or in poor health, you really cannot do your best on the exam. You can come back and take the test some other time.

VII. AT THE TEST

The day of the test is here and you have the test booklet in your hand. The temptation to get going is very strong. Caution! There is more to success than knowing the right answers. You must know how to identify your papers and understand variations in the type of short-answer question used in this particular examination. Follow these suggestions for maximum results from your efforts:

1) Cooperate with the monitor

The test administrator has a duty to create a situation in which you can be as much at ease as possible. He will give instructions, tell you when to begin, check to see that you are marking your answer sheet correctly, and so on. He is not there to guard you, although he will see that your competitors do not take unfair advantage. He wants to help you do your best.

2) Listen to all instructions

Don't jump the gun! Wait until you understand all directions. In most civil service tests you get more time than you need to answer the questions. So don't be in a hurry. Read each word of instructions until you clearly understand the meaning. Study the examples, listen to all announcements and follow directions. Ask questions if you do not understand what to do.

3) Identify your papers

Civil service exams are usually identified by number only. You will be assigned a number; you must not put your name on your test papers. Be sure to copy your number correctly. Since more than one exam may be given, copy your exact examination title.

4) Plan your time

Unless you are told that a test is a "speed" or "rate of work" test, speed itself is usually not important. Time enough to answer all the questions will be provided, but this does not mean that you have all day. An overall time limit has been set. Divide the total time (in minutes) by the number of questions to determine the approximate time you have for each question.

5) Do not linger over difficult questions

If you come across a difficult question, mark it with a paper clip (useful to have along) and come back to it when you have been through the booklet. One caution if you do this – be sure to skip a number on your answer sheet as well. Check often to be sure that you have not lost your place and that you are marking in the row numbered the same as the question you are answering.

6) Read the questions

Be sure you know what the question asks! Many capable people are unsuccessful because they failed to *read* the questions correctly.

7) Answer all questions

Unless you have been instructed that a penalty will be deducted for incorrect answers, it is better to guess than to omit a question.

8) Speed tests

It is often better NOT to guess on speed tests. It has been found that on timed tests people are tempted to spend the last few seconds before time is called in marking answers at random – without even reading them – in the hope of picking up a few extra points. To discourage this practice, the instructions may warn you that your score will be "corrected" for guessing. That is, a penalty will be applied. The incorrect answers will be deducted from the correct ones, or some other penalty formula will be used.

9) Review your answers

If you finish before time is called, go back to the questions you guessed or omitted to give them further thought. Review other answers if you have time.

10) Return your test materials

If you are ready to leave before others have finished or time is called, take ALL your materials to the monitor and leave quietly. Never take any test material with you. The monitor can discover whose papers are not complete, and taking a test booklet may be grounds for disqualification.

VIII. EXAMINATION TECHNIQUES

1) Read the general instructions carefully. These are usually printed on the first page of the exam booklet. As a rule, these instructions refer to the timing of the examination; the fact that you should not start work until the signal and must stop work at a signal, etc. If there are any *special* instructions, such as a choice of questions to be answered, make sure that you note this instruction carefully.

2) When you are ready to start work on the examination, that is as soon as the signal has been given, read the instructions to each question booklet, underline any key words or phrases, such as *least, best, outline, describe* and the like. In this way you will tend to answer as requested rather than discover on reviewing your paper that you *listed without describing*, that you selected the *worst* choice rather than the *best* choice, etc.

3) If the examination is of the objective or multiple-choice type – that is, each question will also give a series of possible answers: A, B, C or D, and you are called upon to select the best answer and write the letter next to that answer on your answer paper – it is advisable to start answering each question in turn. There may be anywhere from 50 to 100 such questions in the three or four hours allotted and you can see how much time would be taken if you read through all the questions before beginning to answer any. Furthermore, if you come across a question or group of questions which you know would be difficult to answer, it would undoubtedly affect your handling of all the other questions.

4) If the examination is of the essay type and contains but a few questions, it is a moot point as to whether you should read all the questions before starting to answer any one. Of course, if you are given a choice – say five out of seven and the like – then it is essential to read all the questions so you can eliminate the two that are most difficult. If, however, you are asked to answer all the questions, there may be danger in trying to answer the easiest one first because you may find that you will spend too much time on it. The best technique is to answer the first question, then proceed to the second, etc.

5) Time your answers. Before the exam begins, write down the time it started, then add the time allowed for the examination and write down the time it must be completed, then divide the time available somewhat as follows:

- If 3-1/2 hours are allowed, that would be 210 minutes. If you have 80 objective-type questions, that would be an average of 2-1/2 minutes per question. Allow yourself no more than 2 minutes per question, or a total of 160 minutes, which will permit about 50 minutes to review.
- If for the time allotment of 210 minutes there are 7 essay questions to answer, that would average about 30 minutes a question. Give yourself only 25 minutes per question so that you have about 35 minutes to review.

6) The most important instruction is to *read each question* and make sure you know what is wanted. The second most important instruction is to *time yourself properly* so that you answer every question. The third most important instruction is to *answer every question*. Guess if you have to but include something for each question. Remember that you will receive no credit for a blank and will probably receive some credit if you write something in answer to an essay question. If you guess a letter – say "B" for a multiple-choice question – you may have guessed right. If you leave a blank as an answer to a multiple-choice question, the examiners may respect your feelings but it will not add a point to your score. Some exams may penalize you for wrong answers, so in such cases *only*, you may not want to guess unless you have some basis for your answer.

7) Suggestions
   a. Objective-type questions
      1. Examine the question booklet for proper sequence of pages and questions
      2. Read all instructions carefully
      3. Skip any question which seems too difficult; return to it after all other questions have been answered
      4. Apportion your time properly; do not spend too much time on any single question or group of questions
      5. Note and underline key words – *all, most, fewest, least, best, worst, same, opposite,* etc.
      6. Pay particular attention to negatives
      7. Note unusual option, e.g., unduly long, short, complex, different or similar in content to the body of the question
      8. Observe the use of "hedging" words – *probably, may, most likely,* etc.
      9. Make sure that your answer is put next to the same number as the question
      10. Do not second-guess unless you have good reason to believe the second answer is definitely more correct
      11. Cross out original answer if you decide another answer is more accurate; do not erase until you are ready to hand your paper in
      12. Answer all questions; guess unless instructed otherwise
      13. Leave time for review

   b. Essay questions
      1. Read each question carefully
      2. Determine exactly what is wanted. Underline key words or phrases.
      3. Decide on outline or paragraph answer

4. Include many different points and elements unless asked to develop any one or two points or elements
5. Show impartiality by giving pros and cons unless directed to select one side only
6. Make and write down any assumptions you find necessary to answer the questions
7. Watch your English, grammar, punctuation and choice of words
8. Time your answers; don't crowd material

8) Answering the essay question

Most essay questions can be answered by framing the specific response around several key words or ideas. Here are a few such key words or ideas:

M's: manpower, materials, methods, money, management
P's: purpose, program, policy, plan, procedure, practice, problems, pitfalls, personnel, public relations
   a. Six basic steps in handling problems:
      1. Preliminary plan and background development
      2. Collect information, data and facts
      3. Analyze and interpret information, data and facts
      4. Analyze and develop solutions as well as make recommendations
      5. Prepare report and sell recommendations
      6. Install recommendations and follow up effectiveness

   b. Pitfalls to avoid
      1. *Taking things for granted* – A statement of the situation does not necessarily imply that each of the elements is necessarily true; for example, a complaint may be invalid and biased so that all that can be taken for granted is that a complaint has been registered
      2. *Considering only one side of a situation* – Wherever possible, indicate several alternatives and then point out the reasons you selected the best one
      3. *Failing to indicate follow up* – Whenever your answer indicates action on your part, make certain that you will take proper follow-up action to see how successful your recommendations, procedures or actions turn out to be
      4. *Taking too long in answering any single question* – Remember to time your answers properly

IX. AFTER THE TEST

Scoring procedures differ in detail among civil service jurisdictions although the general principles are the same. Whether the papers are hand-scored or graded by machine we have described, they are nearly always graded by number. That is, the person who marks the paper knows only the number – never the name – of the applicant. Not until all the papers have been graded will they be matched with names. If other tests, such as training and experience or oral interview ratings have been given, scores will be combined. Different parts of the examination usually have different weights. For example, the written test might count 60 percent of the final grade, and a rating of training and experience 40 percent. In many jurisdictions, veterans will have a certain number of points added to their grades.

After the final grade has been determined, the names are placed in grade order and an eligible list is established. There are various methods for resolving ties between those who get the same final grade – probably the most common is to place first the name of the person whose application was received first. Job offers are made from the eligible list in the order the names appear on it. You will be notified of your grade and your rank as soon as all these computations have been made. This will be done as rapidly as possible.

People who are found to meet the requirements in the announcement are called "eligibles." Their names are put on a list of eligible candidates. An eligible's chances of getting a job depend on how high he stands on this list and how fast agencies are filling jobs from the list.

When a job is to be filled from a list of eligibles, the agency asks for the names of people on the list of eligibles for that job. When the civil service commission receives this request, it sends to the agency the names of the three people highest on this list. Or, if the job to be filled has specialized requirements, the office sends the agency the names of the top three persons who meet these requirements from the general list.

The appointing officer makes a choice from among the three people whose names were sent to him. If the selected person accepts the appointment, the names of the others are put back on the list to be considered for future openings.

That is the rule in hiring from all kinds of eligible lists, whether they are for typist, carpenter, chemist, or something else. For every vacancy, the appointing officer has his choice of any one of the top three eligibles on the list. This explains why the person whose name is on top of the list sometimes does not get an appointment when some of the persons lower on the list do. If the appointing officer chooses the second or third eligible, the No. 1 eligible does not get a job at once, but stays on the list until he is appointed or the list is terminated.

X. HOW TO PASS THE INTERVIEW TEST

The examination for which you applied requires an oral interview test. You have already taken the written test and you are now being called for the interview test – the final part of the formal examination.

You may think that it is not possible to prepare for an interview test and that there are no procedures to follow during an interview. Our purpose is to point out some things you can do in advance that will help you and some good rules to follow and pitfalls to avoid while you are being interviewed.

What is an interview supposed to test?
The written examination is designed to test the technical knowledge and competence of the candidate; the oral is designed to evaluate intangible qualities, not readily measured otherwise, and to establish a list showing the relative fitness of each candidate – as measured against his competitors – for the position sought. Scoring is not on the basis of "right" and "wrong," but on a sliding scale of values ranging from "not passable" to "outstanding." As a matter of fact, it is possible to achieve a relatively low score without a single "incorrect" answer because of evident weakness in the qualities being measured.

Occasionally, an examination may consist entirely of an oral test – either an individual or a group oral. In such cases, information is sought concerning the technical knowledges and abilities of the candidate, since there has been no written examination for this purpose. More commonly, however, an oral test is used to supplement a written examination.

Who conducts interviews?

The composition of oral boards varies among different jurisdictions. In nearly all, a representative of the personnel department serves as chairman. One of the members of the board may be a representative of the department in which the candidate would work. In some cases, "outside experts" are used, and, frequently, a businessman or some other representative of the general public is asked to serve. Labor and management or other special groups may be represented. The aim is to secure the services of experts in the appropriate field.

However the board is composed, it is a good idea (and not at all improper or unethical) to ascertain in advance of the interview who the members are and what groups they represent. When you are introduced to them, you will have some idea of their backgrounds and interests, and at least you will not stutter and stammer over their names.

What should be done before the interview?

While knowledge about the board members is useful and takes some of the surprise element out of the interview, there is other preparation which is more substantive. It *is* possible to prepare for an oral interview – in several ways:

1) Keep a copy of your application and review it carefully before the interview

This may be the only document before the oral board, and the starting point of the interview. Know what education and experience you have listed there, and the sequence and dates of all of it. Sometimes the board will ask you to review the highlights of your experience for them; you should not have to hem and haw doing it.

2) Study the class specification and the examination announcement

Usually, the oral board has one or both of these to guide them. The qualities, characteristics or knowledges required by the position sought are stated in these documents. They offer valuable clues as to the nature of the oral interview. For example, if the job involves supervisory responsibilities, the announcement will usually indicate that knowledge of modern supervisory methods and the qualifications of the candidate as a supervisor will be tested. If so, you can expect such questions, frequently in the form of a hypothetical situation which you are expected to solve. NEVER go into an oral without knowledge of the duties and responsibilities of the job you seek.

3) Think through each qualification required

Try to visualize the kind of questions you would ask if you were a board member. How well could you answer them? Try especially to appraise your own knowledge and background in each area, *measured against the job sought*, and identify any areas in which you are weak. Be critical and realistic – do not flatter yourself.

4) Do some general reading in areas in which you feel you may be weak

For example, if the job involves supervision and your past experience has NOT, some general reading in supervisory methods and practices, particularly in the field of human relations, might be useful. Do NOT study agency procedures or detailed manuals. The oral board will be testing your understanding and capacity, not your memory.

5) Get a good night's sleep and watch your general health and mental attitude

You will want a clear head at the interview. Take care of a cold or any other minor ailment, and of course, no hangovers.

What should be done on the day of the interview?

Now comes the day of the interview itself. Give yourself plenty of time to get there. Plan to arrive somewhat ahead of the scheduled time, particularly if your appointment is in the fore part of the day. If a previous candidate fails to appear, the board might be ready for you a bit early. By early afternoon an oral board is almost invariably behind schedule if there are many candidates, and you may have to wait. Take along a book or magazine to read, or your application to review, but leave any extraneous material in the waiting room when you go in for your interview. In any event, relax and compose yourself.

The matter of dress is important. The board is forming impressions about you – from your experience, your manners, your attitude, and your appearance. Give your personal appearance careful attention. Dress your best, but not your flashiest. Choose conservative, appropriate clothing, and be sure it is immaculate. This is a business interview, and your appearance should indicate that you regard it as such. Besides, being well groomed and properly dressed will help boost your confidence.

Sooner or later, someone will call your name and escort you into the interview room. *This is it.* From here on you are on your own. It is too late for any more preparation. But remember, you asked for this opportunity to prove your fitness, and you are here because your request was granted.

What happens when you go in?

The usual sequence of events will be as follows: The clerk (who is often the board stenographer) will introduce you to the chairman of the oral board, who will introduce you to the other members of the board. Acknowledge the introductions before you sit down. Do not be surprised if you find a microphone facing you or a stenotypist sitting by. Oral interviews are usually recorded in the event of an appeal or other review.

Usually the chairman of the board will open the interview by reviewing the highlights of your education and work experience from your application – primarily for the benefit of the other members of the board, as well as to get the material into the record. Do not interrupt or comment unless there is an error or significant misinterpretation; if that is the case, do not hesitate. But do not quibble about insignificant matters. Also, he will usually ask you some question about your education, experience or your present job – partly to get you to start talking and to establish the interviewing "rapport." He may start the actual questioning, or turn it over to one of the other members. Frequently, each member undertakes the questioning on a particular area, one in which he is perhaps most competent, so you can expect each member to participate in the examination. Because time is limited, you may also expect some rather abrupt switches in the direction the questioning takes, so do not be upset by it. Normally, a board member will not pursue a single line of questioning unless he discovers a particular strength or weakness.

After each member has participated, the chairman will usually ask whether any member has any further questions, then will ask you if you have anything you wish to add. Unless you are expecting this question, it may floor you. Worse, it may start you off on an extended, extemporaneous speech. The board is not usually seeking more information. The question is principally to offer you a last opportunity to present further qualifications or to indicate that you have nothing to add. So, if you feel that a significant qualification or characteristic has been overlooked, it is proper to point it out in a sentence or so. Do not compliment the board on the thoroughness of their examination – they have been sketchy, and you know it. If you wish, merely say, "No thank you, I have nothing further to add." This is a point where you can "talk yourself out" of a good impression or fail to present an important bit of information. Remember, *you close the interview yourself.*

The chairman will then say, "That is all, Mr. _____, thank you." Do not be startled; the interview is over, and quicker than you think. Thank him, gather your belongings and take your leave. Save your sigh of relief for the other side of the door.

How to put your best foot forward

Throughout this entire process, you may feel that the board individually and collectively is trying to pierce your defenses, seek out your hidden weaknesses and embarrass and confuse you. Actually, this is not true. They are obliged to make an appraisal of your qualifications for the job you are seeking, and they want to see you in your best light. Remember, they must interview all candidates and a non-cooperative candidate may become a failure in spite of their best efforts to bring out his qualifications. Here are 15 suggestions that will help you:

1) Be natural – Keep your attitude confident, not cocky

If you are not confident that you can do the job, do not expect the board to be. Do not apologize for your weaknesses, try to bring out your strong points. The board is interested in a positive, not negative, presentation. Cockiness will antagonize any board member and make him wonder if you are covering up a weakness by a false show of strength.

2) Get comfortable, but don't lounge or sprawl

Sit erectly but not stiffly. A careless posture may lead the board to conclude that you are careless in other things, or at least that you are not impressed by the importance of the occasion. Either conclusion is natural, even if incorrect. Do not fuss with your clothing, a pencil or an ashtray. Your hands may occasionally be useful to emphasize a point; do not let them become a point of distraction.

3) Do not wisecrack or make small talk

This is a serious situation, and your attitude should show that you consider it as such. Further, the time of the board is limited – they do not want to waste it, and neither should you.

4) Do not exaggerate your experience or abilities

In the first place, from information in the application or other interviews and sources, the board may know more about you than you think. Secondly, you probably will not get away with it. An experienced board is rather adept at spotting such a situation, so do not take the chance.

5) If you know a board member, do not make a point of it, yet do not hide it

Certainly you are not fooling him, and probably not the other members of the board. Do not try to take advantage of your acquaintanceship – it will probably do you little good.

6) Do not dominate the interview

Let the board do that. They will give you the clues – do not assume that you have to do all the talking. Realize that the board has a number of questions to ask you, and do not try to take up all the interview time by showing off your extensive knowledge of the answer to the first one.

7) Be attentive

You only have 20 minutes or so, and you should keep your attention at its sharpest throughout. When a member is addressing a problem or question to you, give him your undivided attention. Address your reply principally to him, but do not exclude the other board members.

8) Do not interrupt

A board member may be stating a problem for you to analyze. He will ask you a question when the time comes. Let him state the problem, and wait for the question.

9) Make sure you understand the question

Do not try to answer until you are sure what the question is. If it is not clear, restate it in your own words or ask the board member to clarify it for you. However, do not haggle about minor elements.

10) Reply promptly but not hastily

A common entry on oral board rating sheets is "candidate responded readily," or "candidate hesitated in replies." Respond as promptly and quickly as you can, but do not jump to a hasty, ill-considered answer.

11) Do not be peremptory in your answers

A brief answer is proper – but do not fire your answer back. That is a losing game from your point of view. The board member can probably ask questions much faster than you can answer them.

12) Do not try to create the answer you think the board member wants

He is interested in what kind of mind you have and how it works – not in playing games. Furthermore, he can usually spot this practice and will actually grade you down on it.

13) Do not switch sides in your reply merely to agree with a board member

Frequently, a member will take a contrary position merely to draw you out and to see if you are willing and able to defend your point of view. Do not start a debate, yet do not surrender a good position. If a position is worth taking, it is worth defending.

14) Do not be afraid to admit an error in judgment if you are shown to be wrong

The board knows that you are forced to reply without any opportunity for careful consideration. Your answer may be demonstrably wrong. If so, admit it and get on with the interview.

15) Do not dwell at length on your present job

The opening question may relate to your present assignment. Answer the question but do not go into an extended discussion. You are being examined for a *new* job, not your present one. As a matter of fact, try to phrase ALL your answers in terms of the job for which you are being examined.

Basis of Rating

Probably you will forget most of these "do's" and "don'ts" when you walk into the oral interview room. Even remembering them all will not ensure you a passing grade. Perhaps you did not have the qualifications in the first place. But remembering them will help you to put your best foot forward, without treading on the toes of the board members.

Rumor and popular opinion to the contrary notwithstanding, an oral board wants you to make the best appearance possible. They know you are under pressure – but they also want to see how you respond to it as a guide to what your reaction would be under the pressures of the job you seek. They will be influenced by the degree of poise you display, the personal traits you show and the manner in which you respond.

ABOUT THIS BOOK

This book contains tests divided into Examination Sections. Go through each test, answering every question in the margin. At the end of each test look at the answer key and check your answers. On the ones you got wrong, look at the right answer choice and learn. Do not fill in the answers first. Do not memorize the questions and answers, but understand the answer and principles involved. On your test, the questions will likely be different from the samples. Questions are changed and new ones added. If you understand these past questions you should have success with any changes that arise. Tests may consist of several types of questions. We have additional books on each subject should more study be advisable or necessary for you. Finally, the more you study, the better prepared you will be. This book is intended to be the last thing you study before you walk into the examination room. Prior study of relevant texts is also recommended. NLC publishes some of these in our Fundamental Series. Knowledge and good sense are important factors in passing your exam. Good luck also helps. So now study this Passbook, absorb the material contained within and take that knowledge into the examination. Then do your best to pass that exam.

EXAMINATION SECTION

EXAMINATION SECTION
TEST 1

DIRECTIONS: Each question or incomplete statement is followed by several suggested answers or completions. Select the one that BEST answers the question or completes the statement. *PRINT THE LETTER OF THE CORRECT ANSWER IN THE SPACE AT THE RIGHT.*

1. The current trend among MOST ecologists is to consider the coastal zones of America   1.____

   A. a group of diverse, stable ecosystems whose respective managements require a variety of individual approaches
   B. systems that are unique to this continent and require an entirely different set of management techniques from other continental coast zones
   C. a group of unstable ecosystems whose already fragile balance has been destroyed by modern industrial practices
   D. a single natural ecosystem requiring integration of management techniques

2. Of the following methods for controlling industrial particulate discharge into the air, the one which has the GREATEST potential efficiency is   2.____

   A. wet scrubbing
   B. fabric filter bag house
   C. electrostatic precipitation
   D. cyclone filter

3. The process by which objects or solid materials are removed from a water supply is called   3.____

   A. straining   B. treatment
   C. screening   D. precipitating

4. All of the following are generally considered obstacles to United States air quality control operations EXCEPT   4.____

   A. high number of uncertain cause-effect relationships
   B. resistance from industrial operations
   C. little danger perceived by the public
   D. relatively small number of particulate contaminants that have been identified

5. The MOST critical step in any given industrial waste management program is the   5.____

   A. phase separation   B. preliminary investigation
   C. process modification   D. contaminant removal

6. The one of the following that is NOT an option for the control of coastal management offered by the Federal Coastal Management Program is   6.____

   A. direct state control
   B. local control subject to state review
   C. local control consistent with state standards
   D. regional control based upon state collaboration

7. The process through which gaseous contaminants are removed from the air is called   7.____

   A. desorption   B. adsorption
   C. distillation   D. precipitation

8. An automobile's catalytic converter is designed to keep all of the following contaminants   8.____
   from being discharged into the air EXCEPT

   A. lead   B. carbon monoxide
   C. hydrocarbons   D. nitrogen oxides

9. Which of the following is a chemical process of waste-water treatment?   9.____

   A. Screening   B. Distillation
   C. Sedimentation   D. Coagulation

10. The stage that occurs LAST in the treatment process of sanitary sewage is   10.____

    A. sedimentation
    B. screening out solids
    C. biological oxidation
    D. filtering through grit chambers

11. The element of air quality control that can be monitored but NOT managed is   11.____

    A. regulatory standards
    B. emissions
    C. meteorology and dispersion
    D. air quality

12. Currently, the rationale behind MOST water quality control operations is   12.____

    A. public health
    B. aesthetic qualities of water resource
    C. protection of aquatic life
    D. preserving recreational capabilities of water resource

13. In the process of air quality improvement, the practice used as a precleaning process   13.____
    before more efficient methods are applied is called

    A. electrostatic precipitation
    B. mechanical cleaning
    C. gas conditioning
    D. process modifications

14. Which of the following practiced methods for desaliniza-tion of water makes use of a salt-   14.____
    filtering membrane?

    A. Freezing   B. Distillation
    C. Reverse osmosis   D. Electrodialysis

15. The FUNDAMENTAL criterion for managing coastal basins is the   15.____

    A. geological configuration of the basin
    B. depth of the basin
    C. ecological vitality of the system
    D. degree of water exchange or flushing rate

16. The LEAST desirable method for heating gases that are intended to be released from an air cleaning unit is by

    A. direct combustion
    B. heat exchangers
    C. indirect heating of ambient air
    D. cooling entering gases

16.____

17. Of the following stages of conventional wastewater treatment, the one that occurs FIRST is

    A. chlorination   B. sedimentation
    C. oxidation   D. discharge

17.____

18. The air quality control devices capable of removing BOTH particulate and gaseous contaminants from the air are

    A. cyclone filters   B. wet scrubbers
    C. adsorbers   D. filter baghouses

18.____

19. The process of restoration is considered acceptable by MOST ecologists if it is implemented to

    A. compensate for an operation that has been projected as being harmful
    B. correct inadvertent harm or past problems
    C. mitigate the damage in advance of a harmful practice
    D. improve the aesthetics of an environment that is near development

19.____

20. Turbidity, or ultrafine particle solids in a water supply, are PRIMARILY removed through the process of

    A. screening   B. distillation
    C. coagulation   D. oxidation

20.____

21. The object of chemical removal processes in air quality control is to

    A. convert gases to particulate matter
    B. increase the water saturation point of the air medium
    C. convert gases into innocuous chemical compounds
    D. vaporize particulate matter

21.____

22. Which of the following is NOT a practice associated with the restoration of silt-polluted coastal basins?

    A. Limiting dredging to active vegetative periods
    B. Construction of bulkheads along the shore
    C. Implementation of soil conservation practices in adjacent farmlands
    D. Diversion of runoff waters from basin

22.____

23. _____ standards are applied to municipal water control operations to specify the MAXIMUM concentration of certain constituents of a given water supply,

    A. Procedural   B. Performance
    C. Investigation   D. Design

23.____

24. Which of the following is NOT among the most effective methods for the prevention of aquifer contamination?   24.____

    A. Industrial zoning
    B. Strict chemical storage rules
    C. Trenching
    D. Watershed protection

25. Of the following, the chemical process that is NOT considered a control mechanism for air quality is   25.____

    A. masking   B. particulate conversion
    C. reduction   D. oxidation

KEY (CORRECT ANSWERS)

1.	D		11.	C
2.	C		12.	C
3.	C		13.	B
4.	C		14.	C
5.	B		15.	D
6.	D		16.	A
7.	B		17.	B
8.	A		18.	B
9.	D		19.	B
10.	C		20.	C

21.	A
22.	A
23.	B
24.	C
25.	A

TEST 2

DIRECTIONS: DIRECTIONS: Each question or incomplete statement is followed by several suggested answers or completions. Select the one that BEST answers the question or completes the statement. *PRINT THE LETTER OF THE CORRECT ANSWER IN THE SPACE AT THE RIGHT.*

1. The term for the process that removes algae or turbidity from a water supply during the water treatment process is

   A. screening
   C. treatment
   B. straining
   D. discharge

   1.____

2. The method for treating groundwater contamination MOST often used for drinking water supplies is _____ treatment.

   A. chemical
   C. aerobic biological
   B. carbon
   D. ozonation/radiation

   2.____

3. Which of the following is NOT one of the primary factors determining the operation of coastal basin management?

   A. Circulation type
   C. Geology
   B. Climate
   D. Depth

   3.____

4. All of the following are practical methods for limiting the discharge of sulfur oxides into the air EXCEPT

   A. desulfurization of oil
   B. limiting coal use to low-sulfur varieties
   C. removal of sulfur from industrial water supplies
   D. removal of sulfur from coal

   4.____

5. The one of the following that is NOT a practice associated with the construction of spoil islands that will protect marina sites in coastal waters is

   A. vegetation with both upland plants and marsh grasses
   B. avoidance of existing vital areas
   C. constructing elliptical islands parallel to water flow
   D. use of fine soil materials in construction

   5.____

6. The FIRST step in any water quality control procedure is

   A. determination of the plant site
   B. compilation of data needed to reach sound decisions about objectives
   C. imposing immediate short-term controls on water quality
   D. establishment of design standards for plant operations

   6.____

7. Of the following methods for controlling industrial particulate discharge into the air, the one that makes use of gravitational forces is

   A. wet scrubbing
   B. fabric filter bag house
   C. electrostatic precipitation
   D. cyclone filter

   7.____

8. An example of a physical process of wastewater treatment is   8._____

    A. coagulation   B. distillation
    C. ion exchange   D. pH adjustment

9. The type of marine environment that is considered to be MOST in need of management   9._____
is the

    A. lagoon   B. bay
    C. ocean   D. tidal river

10. Of the practiced methods for desalinization of water, the MOST widely used in the United   10._____
States is

    A. freezing   B. distillation
    C. reverse osmosis   D. electrodialysis

11. Each of the following is a noncrystalline adsorbent used to remove contaminants from   11._____
the air EXCEPT

    A. metallic oxides   B. activated carbon
    C. silica gel   D. D, activated alumina

12. The guiding practice of a shorelands management operation is   12._____

    A. excavating drainage canals
    B. clearing vegetation
    C. maintaining natural drainage and stream flow
    D. covering land with impervious surfaces

13. In water treatment, the mixing process during which particles form into aggregate   13._____
masses that settle out is called

    A. osmosis   B. flocculation
    C. straining   D. oxidation

14. The type of standards applied to municipal water control operations that specify the   14._____
required characteristics of a given water supply are _____ standards.

    A. design   B. performance
    C. procedural   D. investigation

15. _____ standards are applied to municipal water control operations that define the   15._____
approaches and methods followed in water quality control activities.

    A. Procedural   B. Design
    C. Investigation   D. Performance

16. Marsh-grass plantings are widely used near coastal waters for all of the following pur-   16._____
poses EXCEPT

    A. stabilizing dredge spoil
    B. creation of marshes
    C. revitalization of microorganisms
    D. creation of alternative bulkheads

17. Which of the following has NOT been widely attempted as a method for the control of automotive emissions?   17.____

    A. Reduction of automobile traffic in urban areas
    B. Altering the composition of motor fuels
    C. Filtering or converting devices for emissions
    D. Modification of the conventional engine

18. The guiding factor for what is an acceptable MINIMUM flow into coastal ecosystems is the   18.____

    A. sedimentation of inlet basin
    B. strength of tidal backflow
    C. critical survival point for microorganisms
    D. dry-season low flows under natural conditions

19. In preparing water that is to be considered drinkable, the PRIMARY method for odor prevention is   19.____

    A. chlorine-ammonia treatment
    B. fluoridation
    C. flocculation
    D. filtration

20. The MOST effective method for containing a contaminant leakage plume that has deeply penetrated an underground water source is   20.____

    A. trenching
    B. installing a clay barrier
    C. well pumping
    D. chemical or biological treatment

21. The ULTIMATE goal of the 1972 Amendment to the Water Pollution Control Act was   21.____

    A. enforceable standards limiting industrial waste disposal practices in United States waters
    B. total elimination of the discharge of pollutants into navigable United States waters
    C. banning of the production and marketing of harmful water pollutants
    D. elimination of water pollutants categorized as *most dangerous* by the Environmental Protection Agency

22. The process by which contaminant chemicals are removed during the water treatment process is called   22.____

    A. screening   B. sedimentation
    C. straining   D. treatment

23. All of the following are aspects of major concern in the protection of coastal basins EXCEPT   23.____

    A. changes in circulation caused by alteration of basin configuration
    B. degradation of ecological condition of basin and its margins
    C. loss of ecologically vital areas
    D. salinity of basin waters

24. The process of lime coagulation is used to remove _____ from a water supply.   24.____

    A. phosphates   B. lead
    C. nitrates   D. iron

25. Of the following, the LEAST effective method for controlling the effect of automotive   25.____
emissions has been

    A. parking restrictions in urban areas
    B. carpooling incentives
    C. modification of liquid fuels
    D. toll bridges and highways

———

KEY (CORRECT ANSWERS)

1.	B	11.	A
2.	B	12.	C
3.	B	13.	B
4.	C	14.	A
5.	D	15.	A
6.	B	16.	C
7.	D	17.	D
8.	B	18.	D
9.	A	19.	A
10.	B	20.	C

21.	B
22.	D
23.	D
24.	A
25.	C

———

EXAMINATION SECTION
TEST 1

DIRECTIONS: Each question or incomplete statement is followed by several suggested answers or completions. Select the one that BEST answers the question or completes the statement. *PRINT THE LETTER OF THE CORRECT ANSWER IN THE SPACE AT THE RIGHT.*

1. The MOST efficient devices to measure the gaseous pollutant content of an air sample are   1._____

   A. cyclones   B. filters
   C. bubblers   D. settling chambers

2. The source MOST likely to cause high concentrations of toxic metals associated with nonpoint source water pollution is   2._____

   A. construction   B. highway de-icing
   C. on-site sewage disposal   D. urban storm runoff

3. In the United States, the required landfill space per person each year is GENERALLY   3._____

   A. ten cubic feet   B. one cubic yard
   C. one cubic acre   D. ten square feet

4. The easiest and most effective method for controlling air pollution is   4._____

   A. source correction   B. treatment
   C. collection   D. dispersion

5. The MOST serious source of air pollution associated with the automobile is the   5._____

   A. fuel tank   B. carburetor
   C. crankcase   D. exhaust

6. Which of the following practices or devices is considered to be a collection or treatment control for urban storm-water runoff?   6._____

   A. Anti-littering laws   B. Street cleaning
   C. Floodplain zoning   D. Detention systems

7. The increasing trend in solid waste disposal in the United States is toward the practice of   7._____

   A. incineration
   B. ocean dumping
   C. sanitary landfill
   D. recycling/resource reclamation

8. The MOST widely practiced method for cooling air pollutants before they reach control equipment is   8._____

   A. dilution   B. settling
   C. heat exchange coils   D. quenching

9. Which of the following is NOT a factor of required knowledge for solving an upgrade problem in wastewater treatment plants?   9._____

A. Staffing pattern
B. Normal operational and maintenance procedures
C. Daily peak flow rates
D. Condition of process hardware

10. The category of solid waste that constitutes the GREATEST volume percentage in the United States is   10.____

  A. residential   B. bulky wastes
  C. commercial   D. industrial

11. In current practice, the SIMPLEST test for ozone content of an air sample measures the air's reaction with   11.____

  A. metals with high lead content
  B. rubber
  C. organics
  D. copper

12. High concentrations of acid pollutants associated with nonpoint source water pollution are MOST likely to be contributed by   12.____

  A. non-coal mining   B. air pollution fallout
  C. agriculture   D. forestry

13. Which of the following methods is used by analysts to measure the concentration of hydrocarbons in an air supply?   13.____

  A. Chemical luminescence   B. Flame ionization
  C. Infrared spectrometry   D. High-volume sampling

14. Environmental engineers generally consider _____ to be the BEST cover material for sanitary landfill sites.   14.____

  A. sandy loam   B. clay
  C. gravel   D. silt

15. Deceleration of an automobile is most likely to cause the HIGHEST relative increase in the amount of   15.____

  A. hydrocarbons   B. carbon monoxide
  C. nitrogen oxides   D. lead

16. The _____method for sanitary landfilling involves the distribution of waste into discrete *cells.*   16.____

  A. slope   B. area   C. ramp   D. trench

17. A DISADVANTAGE associated with the use of controlled burning for solid waste disposal is   17.____

  A. consumption of a large amount of resources
  B. lingering contamination of burn site
  C. increased transport costs
  D. large land area required

18. Each of the following is a primary factor in the determination of the area required for a sanitary landfill site EXCEPT   18.____

    A. percent reduction, by compaction, of on-site refuse volume
    B. amount of cover material required
    C. total projected amount of refuse to be delivered
    D. average density of refuse delivered to landfill

19. The method of solid waste disposal that currently involves the GREATEST costs in capital investment is   19.____

    A. incineration   B. ocean dumping
    C. landfilling   D. composting

20. The substance normally used in filters to detect the presence of sulfur dioxide in an air sample is   20.____

    A. microorganisms   B. sulfur
    C. lead peroxide   D. carbon

21. Which of the following is NOT a quality parameter of concern in the activated carbon treatment of wastewater?   21.____

    A. Heavy metals   B. Suspended solids
    C. Trace organics   D. Dissolved oxygen

22. The problem that presents the GREATEST potential hazard to landfill sites is   22.____

    A. pests   B. water pollution
    C. gas   D. decomposition

23. The MOST serious problem associated with the investigative practice of industrial stack sampling is   23.____

    A. control of potentially great capital expense
    B. risk of obtaining an unrepresentative sample
    C. safety risks for analysts
    D. skewing of sample readings by heat concentrations

24. The MOST common method for disinfection in wastewater treatment plants is   24.____

    A. ozone treatment
    B. ultraviolet light exposure
    C. chlorination
    D. introduction of bromine chloride

25. Of the following categories for the pollution control of urban stormwater runoff, _____ controls are considered to be the MOST effective and inexpensive.   25.____

    A. planning   B. accumulation
    C. treatment   D. collection

KEY (CORRECT ANSWERS)

1.	C		11.	B
2.	D		12.	A
3.	B		13.	B
4.	A		14.	A
5.	D		15.	A
6.	D		16.	B
7.	D		17.	C
8.	C		18.	C
9.	C		19.	D
10.	D		20.	C

21. A
22. B
23. B
24. C
25. A

TEST 2

DIRECTIONS: Each question or incomplete statement is followed by several suggested answers or completions. Select the one that BEST answers the question or completes the statement. *PRINT THE LETTER OF THE CORRECT ANSWER IN THE SPACE AT THE RIGHT.*

1. _____% of solid waste in the United States is considered compostible.   1.____

    A. 5-10   B. 20-30   C. 50-75   D. 80-85

2. Which of the following is NOT considered to be a factor affecting the level of organic decomposition in sanitary landfills?   2.____

    A. Moisture   B. Surface area of fill
    C. Temperature   D. Depth of fill

3. The SIMPLEST and MOST widely used device for controlling the particulate content of an air supply is the   3.____

    A. settling chamber   B. adsorber
    C. wet collector   D. bubbler

4. The agricultural practice MOST likely to contribute high levels of total dissolved solids to nonpoint source water pollution is   4.____

    A. animal production
    B. irrigated crop production
    C. pasturing and rangeland
    D. non-irrigated crop production

5. Pathogenic bacteria in wastewater supplies are likely to be produced by each of the following EXCEPT   5.____

    A. construction operations
    B. food processing industries
    C. pharmaceutical manufacturing
    D. tanneries

6. The substance MOST often used to remove sulfur from discharged flue gases is   6.____

    A. copper   B. lime   C. water   D. acid

7. In controlling automotive emissions, an activated carbon canister is used to store emissions from the   7.____

    A. manifold   B. fuel tank
    C. crankcase   D. exhaust

8. Which of the following is NOT a disadvantage associated with the use of sanitary landfill sites for solid waste disposal?   8.____

    A. High collection costs
    B. Jurisdiction entanglements
    C. Large amount of land required
    D. Difficulties presented by seasonal changes

9. The Ringelmann scale is a device used to measure the _____ of an air sample.   9.____

    A. smoke density   B. odor
    C. temperature   D. gaseous pollutant content

10. High-volume sampling is a method for detecting   10.____

    A. ozone   B. oxidant
    C. particulate   D. sulfur dioxide

11. An example of air pollution abatement, as opposed to source control, is   11.____

    A. change of raw material   B. modification of process
    C. equipment modifications   D. stack dispersion

12. *Pollutant loading* is a term that defines the   12.____

    A. collection of pollutants for treatment in a control exercise
    B. quantity of pollution detached and transported into surface watercourses
    C. saturation point of any environment in terms of its pollutant capacity
    D. process of contamination, by an industrial source, of the ambient air

13. Each of the following is an advantage associated with the controlled burning of solid   13.____
wastes EXCEPT

    A. land can be returned to immediate use
    B. sites are longer-lasting
    C. reduced amount of required land
    D. relatively easy collection and transport of materials

14. The device capable of removing the smallest particle from an air supply is the   14.____

    A. electrostatic precipitator
    B. settling chamber
    C. bag filter
    D. wet collector

15. High concentrations of suspended solids associated with nonpoint source water pollution   15.____
are MOST likely contributed by

    A. urban storm runoff
    B. construction
    C. air pollution fallout
    D. non-irrigated crop production

16. Which of the following is NOT one of the primary steps involved in the control of gaseous   16.____
air pollutants?

    A. Removal of pollutant from emissions
    B. Change in process producing pollutant
    C. Dispersion of the pollutant
    D. Chemical conversion of the pollutant

17. To control automotive air pollution, the process of recycling blow-by gases is a method   17.____
for controlling emissions from the

    A. fuel tank   B. exhaust
    C. carburetor   D. crankcase

18. In testing a water supply for the presence of coliform bacteria, the survey method MOST   18.____
likely to be used is

    A. oxygen demand   B. dissolved oxygen
    C. total dissolved solids   D. suspended solids

19. In measuring the constituency of a given air supply, analysts use the process of infrared   19.____
spectrometry to determine concentrations of

    A. oxidants   B. carbon monoxide
    C. sulfur dioxide   D. particulates

20. Which of the following is NOT one of the primary factors affecting the choice of pollution   20.____
control methods for urban stormwater runoff?

    A. Specific constituents of runoff
    B. Type of sewage system
    C. Status of area development
    D. Method of land use

21. A disadvantage associated with the use of sanitary landfill sites for solid waste disposal   21.____
is

    A. high personnel and plant costs
    B. weakened accomodation of peak quantities
    C. potential for groundwater pollution
    D. difficulty with unusual, bulky materials

22. The MOST serious problem in air pollution is presented by   22.____

    A. cooling of pollutants   B. treatment of pollutants
    C. collection of pollutants   D. source modifications

23. Of the following practices or devices, the one considered to be an accumulation control   23.____
for urban stormwater runoff is

    A. automobile inspection   B. street cleaning
    C. floodplain zoning   D. catch basins

24. _____ is used to survey an air sample for the presence of sulfur dioxide.   24.____

    A. Liquid medium   B. Colorimetry
    C. High-volume sampling   D. Flame ionization

25. Acceleration of an automobile is most likely to cause the HIGHEST relative increase in   25.____
the amount of

    A. hydrocarbons   B. carbon monoxide
    C. nitrogen oxides   D. lead

KEY (CORRECT ANSWERS)

1.	D	11.	D
2.	B	12.	B
3.	A	13.	D
4.	B	14.	A
5.	A	15.	B
6.	B	16.	C
7.	B	17.	D
8.	A	18.	A
9.	A	19.	B
10.	C	20.	A

21.	C
22.	C
23.	B
24.	B
25.	C

EXAMINATION SECTION
TEST 1

DIRECTIONS: Each question or incomplete statement is followed by several suggested answers or completions. Select the one that BEST answers the question or completes the statement. *PRINT THE LETTER OF THE CORRECT ANSWER IN THE SPACE AT THE RIGHT.*

1. Which of the following devices has the HIGHEST energy efficiency?   1._____

    A. Diesel engine   B. Small electric motor
    C. Home gas furnace   D. Solar cell

2. A change in the quality of an environment, caused by an increase in temperature, is   2._____
    called

    A. thermal pollution   B. oxidation
    C. thermodynamics   D. transpiration

3. Which of the following industries places the HIGHEST energy demands on the environ-   3._____
    ment?

    A. Food production and processing
    B. Paper and related products
    C. Stone, clay, glass, and concrete production
    D. Chemicals and chemical products

4. The environmental influence responsible for more human illness than any other factor is   4._____

    A. nuclear waste   B. air pollution
    C. acid rain   D. water pollution

5. Which of the following is NOT a difficulty involved in putting wind energy to use?   5._____

    A. Harnessing the three-dimensional dispersion of wind
    B. Finding locations that are consistently windy enough to be useful
    C. Erratic and variable speeds of most winds
    D. Inefficient transmission of energy from collection sites to populations

6. Which of the following classes of insecticides will break down MOST quickly after their   6._____
    use?

    A. Chlorinated hydrocarbons, such as DDT
    B. Botanicals, such as Rotenone
    C. Organophosphates, such as Malathion
    D. Carbamates, such as Sevin

7. In harvesting coal from the earth, the difference between tunnel and strip mining is that   7._____
    strip mining

    A. is more expensive
    B. is less efficient
    C. is more likely to cause soil erosion
    D. disrupts the flow of ground water

8. The MAIN portion of metallic lead toxins are produced by   8._____

    A. paint products   B. automobile emissions
    C. commercial pesticides   D. home electricity

9. What is the common name for a heat pump that heats the exterior at the expense of the   9._____
    interior?

    A. Furnace   B. Generator
    C. Refrigerator   D. Turbine

10. Artificially raising the temperature of aquatic environments has a negative effect on   10._____
    aquatic organisms because

    A. some organisms become infertile at warmer temperatures
    B. warm water carries less oxygen than cold
    C. the mobility of larger organisms is decreased
    D. warm water interferes with the photosynthesis of microorganisms

11. The type of energy source that does NOT add additional heat to the environment is   11._____

    A. solar   B. fossil fuel
    C. hydroelectric   D. tidal

12. Which of the following is NOT a drawback involved with the use of agricultural insecti-   12._____
    cides?

    A. Gradual acquisition of immunity by pest populations
    B. The loss of beneficial insects, such as wasps
    C. Eventual damage to plant matter in crops
    D. Environmental contamination from chemical residues

13. Radiation that arises from natural radioactive materials that are ALWAYS present in the   13._____
    environment is called

    A. background radiation   B. ionizing radiation
    C. backfill   D. alpha radiation

14. The INITIAL factor in the formation of natural oil and gas deposits is   14._____

    A. large accumulations of organic matter
    B. seismic activity beneath the earth"s surface
    C. drying-out of large bodies of water
    D. volcanic mixture of earthly minerals

15. What is the APPROXIMATE percentage of air pollutants, by weight, that come directly   15._____
    from automobiles?

    A. 10%   B. 40%   C. 65%   D. 80%

16. In detergents, the additives that extract minerals from washing water are   16._____

    A. enzymes   B. lyes
    C. phosphates   D. nitrates

17. Which of the following methods of transportation requires the LOWEST expense of energy per person/passenger? 17.____

   A. Walking
   B. Train
   C. Intercity bus
   D. Bicycle

18. Which of the following chemical compounds is a component of acid rain? 18.____

   A. Hydrogen sulfide
   B. Carbon monoxide
   C. Hydrocarbon
   D. Sulfur dioxide

19. Most of the electricity used in the United States today is generated by 19.____

   A. solar cells
   B. tidal generators
   C. steam turbines
   D. internal combustion engines

20. Which of the following methods of municipal waste is MOST harmful to the environment and surrounding populations? 20.____

   A. Open dumping
   B. Sanitary landfill
   C. Incineration
   D. Incineration and ocean dumping

21. Which of the following is NOT a problem posed by the construction of hydroelectric dams? 21.____

   A. Wildlife habitat destruction
   B. Water loss through evaporation
   C. Total obstruction of seasonal water flow
   D. Silting-up of reservoirs

22. Each of the following is a principal constituent of fertilizer runoff EXCEPT 22.____

   A. hydrocarbons
   B. nitrates
   C. potash
   D. phosphates

23. Of the following, which industry is responsible for the GREATEST amount of hazardous wastes imposed upon the environment? 23.____

   A. Organic chemicals, pesticides, and explosives
   B. Pharmaceuticals
   C. Petroleum refining
   D. Smelting and refining of primary metals

24. Which of the following is a non-renewable energy resource? 24.____

   A. Tidal currents
   B. Natural oil/gas deposits
   C. Solar heat
   D. Geothermal energy

25. The suspension of air pollutants in the atmosphere near the earth's surface is caused by 25.____

   A. littoral drift
   B. convection
   C. thermal inversion
   D. acid rain

KEY (CORRECT ANSWERS)

1.	C		11.	A
2.	A		12.	C
3.	D		13.	A
4.	D		14.	A
5.	B		15.	B
6.	B		16.	C
7.	C		17.	D
8.	B		18.	D
9.	C		19.	C
10.	B		20.	A

21.	C
22.	A
23.	A
24.	B
25.	C

TEST 2

DIRECTIONS: Each question or incomplete statement is followed by several suggested answers or completions. Select the one that BEST answers the question or completes the statement. *PRINT THE LETTER OF THE CORRECT ANSWER IN THE SPACE AT THE RIGHT.*

1. Which of the following sources is responsible for the GREATEST level of ozone depletion in the earth's atmosphere?

    A. Aerosol propellants
    B. Commercial and residential refrigeration
    C. Production of plastic foam and insulation
    D. Solvent cleaning of metal and electronic parts

1.____

2. High concentrations of mercury and aluminum in soil are caused by

    A. acid contamination   B. plant respiration
    C. ammonia seepage   D. natural decomposition

2.____

3. Which of the following waste products is MOST abundant in landfill sites?

    A. Paper products   B. Plastics
    C. Glass   D. Metals

3.____

4. Which of the following types of cells are LEAST susceptible to contamination from nuclear waste?

    A. Reproductive   B. Blood
    C. Lymph   D. Nerve

4.____

5. Which of the following effects is caused by the runoff of agricultural fertilizers into surface water supplies?

    A. Sterilization of larger aquatic vertebrates
    B. Killing algae and other microorganisms
    C. Increasing mercury content
    D. Eventual depletion of oxygen

5.____

6. Traditionally, most low-level nuclear wastes produced in the United States have been disposed of

    A. in deep formations of stable rock
    B. under sheets of polar ice
    C. in shallow land-burial sites
    D. far into the open sea

6.____

7. Which of the following is the result of atmospheric decomposition that comes from emissions of sulfur dioxide and oxides of nitrogen?

    A. Ozone depletion   B. Smog
    C. Fermentation   D. Acid rain

7.____

8. Highly toxic chemicals, such as PCBs, that are the byproducts of manufacturing pro-   8._____
cesses or waste-burning are called

    A. hydrocarbons   B. solvents
    C. dioxins   D. fluorocarbons

9. Which of the following is NOT a potential source of fossil fuel?   9._____

    A. Iron ore   B. Tar sand
    C. Shale   D. Underground methane

10. Each of the following is considered an effective material for lining the disposal sites of   10._____
toxic wastes EXCEPT

    A. clay   B. rubber
    C. plastic   D. sandstone

11. Which energy source presents the GREATEST risk to workers involved in the entire pro-   11._____
cess of energy production?

    A. Coal   B. Oil
    C. Natural gas   D. Uranium

12. Water vapor that has collected around microscopic particles of air pollution is described   12._____
as

    A. smog   B. acid rain
    C. haze   D. particulate

13. The PRIMARY stage of municipal sewage treatment removes which of the following ele-   13._____
ments from sewage?

    A. Dissolved chemicals   B. Grit and coarse solids
    C. Sediments   D. Microorganisms

14. Introducing microbes that feed on water contaminants into a polluted body of water is an   14._____
example of

    A. adsorption   B. bioremediation
    C. desalinization   D. integrated pest control

15. Producing energy by splitting the nucleus of a single radioactive atom is called   15._____

    A. radiation   B. nuclear fission
    C. neutron chain reaction   D. nuclear fusion

16. Which of the following is NOT a source of acid precipitation?   16._____

    A. Automobile emissions
    B. Nuclear power generation
    C. Coal-burning stoves
    D. Electrical plants powered by steam turbines

17. Currently, the LEAST plentiful energy source available to the United States from our nat-   17._____
ural reserves is

    A. petroleum   B. natural gas
    C. coal   D. uranium oxide

22

18. Which of the following chemical compounds is a PRIMARY cause of ozone depletion?   18._____

    A. Nitrogen oxide   B. Bicarbonate
    C. Dioxin   D. Chlorofluorocarbon

19. Which of the following is a function performed by a solar collector?   19._____

    A. Heating water
    B. Using sunlight to ignite combustible materials
    C. Converting sunlight to electricity
    D. Storing energy

20. Sulfur dioxide, a poisonous gas, is produced by the   20._____

    A. use of aerosol sprays
    B. evaporation of acid-contaminated waters
    C. burning of coal
    D. upwelling of poorly-contained nuclear wastes

21. Which of the following is an example of *point source* water pollution?   21._____

    A. Agricultural runoff into streams
    B. Seepage of industrial chemicals into groundwater supplies
    C. An oil spill caused by the wreck of a tanker
    D. Acid rain contamination of a large lake

22. Which non-chemical pollutant has proven MOST hazardous to marine and aquatic wild-life?   22._____

    A. Metals   B. Paper products
    C. Plastics   D. Construction by-products

23. Most of the thermoplastics produced in the United States are from which of the following categories?   23._____

    A. Polyethylene   B. Polystyrene
    C. Polypropylene   D. Polyurethane

24. Each of the following is an example of a *soft* energy resource EXCEPT   24._____

    A. geothermal heat   B. wind energy
    C. natural gas deposits   D. solar power

25. Which type of coal has the GREATEST heating potential?   25._____

    A. Bituminous   B. Anthracite
    C. Subbituminous   D. Lignite

KEY (CORRECT ANSWERS)

1.	C		11.	A
2.	A		12.	C
3.	A		13.	B
4.	D		14.	B
5.	D		15.	B
6.	C		16.	B
7.	D		17.	A
8.	C		18.	D
9.	A		19.	A
10.	D		20.	C

21.	C
22.	C
23.	A
24.	C
25.	B

————————

EXAMINATION SECTION
TEST 1

DIRECTIONS: Each question or incomplete statement is followed by several suggested answers or completions. Select the one that BEST answers the question or completes the statement. *PRINT THE LETTER OF THE CORRECT ANSWER IN THE SPACE AT THE RIGHT.*

1.   Which of the following types of parameters is NOT generally considered to be one of the primary factors in defining environmental quality?

    A.   Physical   B.   Meteorological
    C.   Biological   D.   Chemical

1.____

2.   All of the following resources are listed in the National Wildlife Federation's annual Environmental Quality Index EXCEPT

    A.   timber   B.   human population
    C.   minerals   D.   living space

2.____

3.   In dollars, the costs of low air quality in the United States are GREATEST in relation to

    A.   human health   B.   materials
    C.   vegetation   D.   residential property

3.____

4.   Evaluations of soil quality are MOST commonly expressed in terms of

    A.   chemical contamination
    B.   erodibility
    C.   mineral constituency
    D.   use of soluble nitrogen forms

4.____

5.   Of the methods for water quality measurement below, which does NOT measure the effects of a given constituent?

    A.   Threshold odor tests
    B.   Bioassays of live fish
    C.   Tests for chromium concentration
    D.   Tests for *hardness*

5.____

6.   Environmental quality indices are MOST successfully used for

    A.   resource allocation   B.   public information
    C.   scientific research   D.   enforcement of standards

6.____

7.   In conducting water quality assessments intended to reveal the incidence of pathogens, _____ is MOST often the focus.

    A.   nonpathogenic bacteria   B.   ammonia
    C.   microscopic plants   D.   pathogens

7.____

8.   Each of the following is a primary use of air quality data by state and local agencies EXCEPT

8.____

A. determination of compliance with standards
B. reporting daily quality levels to the public
C. determination of critical episodes requiring emer-gency measures
D. enacting quality legislation

9. Of the following units for evaluating the radioactivity of an environment, _____ is a mea-sure of the activity of radioactive materials.

    A. rad   B. dose equivalent
    C. curie   D. roentgen

9._____

10. The one of the following that is NOT a factor in calculat-ing the average soil loss for a given crop rotation is

    A. temperature   B. erosion control practice
    C. rainfall   D. length of slope

10._____

11. Which of the following devices for assessing the quality of a radioactive environment offers the LEAST accurate quantitative measurements?

    A. Counter   B. Ionization chamber
    C. Magnetic filter   D. Photographic film

11._____

12. Solid-media water quality assessments that produce a green substance on the medium indicate

    A. algae   B. coliform bacteria
    C. pathogens   D. chlorine

12._____

13. The MOST important factor in determining the quality of a water resource is the

A. purpose for which the water is being considered
B. flow capacity of the resource
C. chemical purity of the water
D. biotic potential of the resource

13._____

14. According to the National Wildlife Federation's annual Environmental Quality Index, of the United States' resources, _____ is in the BEST relative condition.

    A. timber   B. air   C. water   D. soil

14._____

15. Which of the following is NOT usually a component of quality of life surveys conducted in urban environments?

    A. Political   B. Economic
    C. Ecological   D. Health and education

15._____

16. Approximately _____% of the earth's water supply is drinkable.

    A. .5   B. 1-3   C. 3-5   D. 5-10

16._____

17. A land-use quality index that measures the number of acres lost or gained to wildlife is known as a(n)_____ index.

    A. encroachment   B. overlap
    C. habitat change   D. urban green

17._____

18. Which of the following methods of water quality evaluation is considered a last resort by analysts?   18.____

    A. Measurement of factors associated with a given constituent
    B. Measuring the effects of constituents
    C. Qualitative descriptions
    D. Direct measurement of constituent concentrations

19. _____ is NOT one of the primary impact standards by which air quality is evaluated.   19.____

    A. Esthetic   B. Meteorological
    C. Health   D. Economic

20. The expression of pesticide injury to plants is a function of each of the following EXCEPT   20.____

    A. chemical properties of the pesticide
    B. sorptive ability of soil
    C. soil erodibility
    D. climatic conditions

21. Of the following, experts have developed the LEAST definitive quality index so far for   21.____

    A. total environment   B. air
    C. solid waste   D. water

22. Of the methods for water quality measurement below, which is an example of DIRECT measurement and reportage of a given concentration?   22.____

    A. Determination of the iron content of drinking water
    B. Determining water *hardness*
    C. Measuring alkalinity
    D. Turbidity analysis

23. In order to determine the quality of a solid waste disposal management system, each of the following charac-teristics of solid waste must be measured EXCEPT   23.____

    A. particle size   B. density
    C. chemical makeup   D. waste source

24. _____ is a measure of absorbed radiation dosage.   24.____

    A. Rad   B. Dose equivalent
    C. Roentgen   D. Curie

25. According to the National Wildlife Federation, of the resources given below, _____ has the GREATEST relativeimportance to human life.   25.____

    A. air   B. wildlife   C. soil   D. water

———

KEY (CORRECT ANSWERS)

1.	B		11.	D
2.	B		12.	B
3.	A		13.	A
4.	D		14.	D
5.	C		15.	C
6.	B		16.	A
7.	C		17.	C
8.	D		18.	C
9.	C		19.	B
10.	A		20.	C

21. A
22. A
23. D
24. A
25. C

TEST 2

DIRECTIONS: Each question or incomplete statement is followed by several suggested answers or completions. Select the one that BEST answers the question or completes the statement. *PRINT THE LETTER OF THE CORRECT ANSWER IN THE SPACE AT THE RIGHT.*

1. The appearance of a purple culture in the Gram-stain water quality assessment indicates a _____ result for _____.   1.____

    A. positive; microscopic plants
    B. negative; coliforms
    C. positive; blue-green algae
    D. negative; pathogens

2. The constituent LEAST likely to be measured by an Air Quality Index is   2.____

    A. hydrocarbon
    C. particulate
    B. sulfur dioxide
    D. carbon monoxide

3. A land-use quality index that is limited to assessing *man-made* environments is known as a(n) _____ index.   3.____

    A. encroachment
    C. habitat change
    B. overlap
    D. urban green

4. Which of the following is NOT an example of a quantitative water quality measurement based on an arbitrary scale?   4.____

    A. Suspended solids
    C. Acidity
    B. Volatile solids
    D. Color

5. The degree to which an environment can be considered *natural* is measured PRIMARILY in terms of   5.____

    A. the total species diversity of the environment
    B. the type of management imposed on the environment
    C. the degree to which ecological succession is allowed to take place
    D. its current station in the process of ecological succession

6. The ability of a soil resource to retain nitrogen is a function of each of the following EXCEPT   6.____

    A. altitude
    C. soil texture
    B. aeration
    D. temperature

7. The basis for judging whether a water resource is suitable for the uses under consideration is determined by   7.____

    A. absolute standards of purity and biotic potential that are established locally
    B. comparison of uses with projected capacity of the resource
    C. consensus of the population to be served by the resource
    D. comparison of data with published criteria concerning the purpose of the resource

8. For the sake of simplicity and comprehensiveness, MOST of the Environmental Protection Agency's quality reports take the form of   8.____

A. anecdotal reports
B. bar graphs and charts
C. raw data
D. time series plots

9. In measuring the ecological quality of an environment, which of the following categories   9.____
   of vegetation properties is NOT used as an indicator?

   A. Elemental composition
   B. Morphology
   C. Specific growth rates
   D. Species presence

10. Of the following devices for assessing the quality of a radioactive environment, the one   10.____
    designed to note the movement of single particles through a defined volume is

    A. photographic film
    B. ionization chamber
    C. magnetic filter
    D. counter

11. Of the methods for water quality measurement below, which is an example of a qualita-   11.____
    tive description?

    A. Microbiological content
    B. Floating matter and debris
    C. Turbidity
    D. Mercury concentration limits

12. According to the National Wildlife Federation's annual Environmental Quality Index, of   12.____
    the United States' resources, _____ is in the WORST relative condition.

    A. wildlife   B. air   C. water   D. soil

13. Which of the following factors is NOT usually included in measurements of the effects of   13.____
    environmental noise on humans?

    A. Frequency spectrum
    B. Time variations of frequency and sound level
    C. Noise source
    D. Overall sound level

14. Most analysts agree that an accurate, readable index measuring the quality of a total   14.____
    environment would have to include _____ factors.

    A. fewer than thirty
    B. between forty and seventy
    C. no more than ten
    D. over 100

15. A soil quality index intended for measuring pesticide residue must be a function of each   15.____
    of the following variables EXCEPT

    A. irrigation practices
    B. pesticide
    C. crop
    D. climate

16. The method of water quality measurement considered by analysts to be the quickest and   16.____
    most accurate is

A.   measurement of factors associated with a given constituent
B.   qualitative descriptions
C.   direct measurement of constituent concentrations
D.   measurement of the effects of a given constituent

17.   A land-use quality index that measures the proportion of developed to undeveloped land   17.____
is known as a(n) _____ index.

A.   encroachment   B.   overlap
C.   habitat change   D.   urban green

18.   Which of the following is NOT among the basic uses for environmental quality indices?   18.____

A.   Public information
B.   Ranking of industries by quality level
C.   Ranking of locations by quality level
D.   Trend analysis

19.   The baseline alkalinity concentration criteria for a freshwater resource's ability to support   19.____
aquatic life is generally considered to be _____milligrams per liter.

A.   no more than 10   B.   between 5 and 50
C.   between 0 and 15   D.   no less than 20

20.   In evaluating the quality of a soil resource, the MOST difficult aspect to determine accu-   20.____
rately is

A.   aeration
B.   the form taken by nitrates
C.   moisture content
D.   total nitrogen content

21.   All of the following are main classes of air quality measurements EXCEPT   21.____

A.   ambient air quality   B.   meteorological
C.   radiological   D.   emissions

22.   _____is MOST likely to cause taste and odor problems in a surface water supply.   22.____

A.   Coliform bacteria   B.   Fluoride
C.   Chlorine   D.   Algae

23.   Of the methods for air quality measurement given below, which is used to detect and   23.____
measure the incidence of carbon monoxide?

A.   Infrared spectrometry   B.   Chemical luminescence
C.   Flame ionization   D.   High-volume sampling

24.   Of the methods for water quality measurement below, the one which is NOT an example   24.____
of measuring factors associated with a given constituent is

A.   biochemical oxygen demand
B.   suspended solids measurement
C.   use of total organic carbon
D.   indicator organism tests

25. According to the National Wildlife Federation, of the resources below, _____ has the   25.____
    LEAST relative importance to human life.

    A. air   B. wildlife
    C. minerals   D. living space

KEY (CORRECT ANSWERS)

1.	B		11.	B
2.	A		12.	B
3.	A		13.	C
4.	B		14.	D
5.	C		15.	A
6.	A		16.	A
7.	D		17.	D
8.	B		18.	B
9.	C		19.	D
10.	D		20.	B

21.	C
22.	D
23.	A
24.	B
25.	B

EXAMINATION SECTION
TEST 1

DIRECTIONS: Each question or incomplete statement is followed by several suggested answers or completions. Select the one that BEST answers the question or completes the statement. *PRINT THE LETTER OF THE CORRECT ANSWER IN THE SPACE AT THE RIGHT.*

1. Which of the following devices is considered to be the MOST effective way of reporting a water supply's chemical composition data?   1.____

   A. table   B. bar graph
   C. cross-referenced spread sheet   D. circular graph

2. The type of data report which MUST be used as an integral part of any dataprocessing system associated with air quality measurement is   2.____

   A. data summarization   B. diurnal variation pattern
   C. pollutant rose   D. frequency distribution

3. The term for an analyst's attempt to detect and correct any errors that have entered the data set is data   3.____

   A. handling   B. validation
   C. processing   D. proofing

4. Of the types of data listed below, which one is NOT used as a parameter to define the physical characteristics of a lake?   4.____

   A. Surface area   B. Average depth
   C. Underlying rock characteristics   D. Retention time

5. The difference between the least and greatest values in a data set is known as the set's   5.____

   A. variance   B. range   C. mean deviation   D. mode

6. When experts in the same field disagree about conclusions drawn from a set of environmental impact assessment data, they sometimes privately answer a prepared questionnaire, and then distribute a summary sheet of opposing viewpoints amongst themselves. This method is known as   6.____

   A. the cooperative assessment model
   B. the Delphi technique
   C. the operational gaming model
   D. collective data validation

7. The term for calculated decrease In water pressure within a delivery system is   7.____

   A. vacuum   B. head loss   C. backup   D. flow gradient

8. Of the types of environmental impact data variables below, the one which is an example of an output variable is   8.____

   A. effects on natural and social environments
   B. population projections
   C. transportation networks
   D. economic growth

9. All of the following are factors required for the calculation of flow velocity in water delivery systems EXCEPT   9.____

    A. quantity of flow   B. pipe material
    C. slope of hydraulic gradient   D. temperature of flow

10. _____ errors in a data set are MOST easily estimated by the use of standard statistical techniques.   10.____

    A. Systematic   B. Random   C. Clerical   D. Standard

11. The one of the following which Is NOT an element of the data base needed in order to make decisions about water quality control is the   11.____

    A. physical characteristics of the water resource
    B. local needs and desires concerning use
    C. projected quality of untreated water
    D. present uses of resource

12. The air quality data report that consists of collected averages for a specific daily time period is the   12.____

    A. pollutant rose   B. data summarization
    C. diurnal variation pattern   D. frequency distribution

13. The concentration of bacteriological wastes in water is USUALLY expressed in terms of   13.____

    A. parts per million
    B. specific particle ratios, depending on the waste
    C. kiloPascals
    D. BOD

14. The one of the characteristics below that Is NOT used as a criterion for determining the quality of a data set is   14.____

    A. flexibility   B. representativeness
    C. comparability   D. completeness

15. In water delivery systems, water pressure is USUALLY measured in units called   15.____

    A. meters of head   B. pounds per square inch
    C. flow gradients   D. Pascals

16. In measuring air quality, extremes in data are often due to each of the following EXCEPT   16.____

    A. meteorological factors   B. clerical misrecordings
    C. lab errors   D. saturation of continuous data

17. The term for the difference between a data set's MEASURED and REFERENCED values is   17.____

    A. accuracy   B. quantitative error
    C. reliability   D. precision

18. In order to determine the storage needed to equalize a community's water supply demand at a constant pumping pressure, the MOST important data set needed is the

    A. exact pumping pressure
    B. time of daily peak use
    C. community's consumption rate
    D. delivery time between source and key use stations

18.____

19. _____ is the MOST commonly used method for determining the central value of a given data set.

    A. Mid-range   B. Mode
    C. Arithmetic mean   D. Median

19.____

20. What is the method for determining the standard deviation of values in a data set?

    A. Square root of the variance
    B. Half the total variance
    C. Average of all deviating values
    D. Average of the square roots of all deviating values

20.____

21. The MOST commonly used device for recording and reporting water delivery data at household sites is the

    A. compound meter   B. digital register
    C. current meter   D. disk meter

21.____

22. The term for the air quality data report that summarizes how often concentrations of specific magnitudes occur is

    A. frequency distribution   B. data summarization
    C. pollutant rose   D. diurnal variation pattern

22.____

23. Regarding environmental impact assessment, the goal of relating input and output variables in a data set is to

    A. validate the data set
    B. understand the consequences of imposing alternative policies
    C. establish a consensus about policy objectives
    D. compile an adequately useful data set

23.____

24. In order to calculate the intake capacity for a fire flow water delivery system, an analyst should compare the system's

    A. average pressure to the average distance of delivery
    B. total storage to the maximum amount of water needed
    C. maximum pressure to the maximum distance of delivery
    D. total storage to the average amount of water needed

24.____

25. Which of the distorting factors below is almost EXCLUSIVELY involved with the presentation of data, rather than the documentation?

    A. Mechanical error   B. Bias
    C. Meteorological factors   D. Clerical error

25.____

KEY (CORRECT ANSWERS)

1.	B		11.	C
2.	A		12.	C
3.	B		13.	D
4.	C		14.	A
5.	B		15.	A
6.	B		16.	D
7.	B		17.	A
8.	A		18.	C
9.	D		19.	C
10.	B		20.	A

21.	D
22.	A
23.	B
24.	B
25.	B

———

TEST 2

DIRECTIONS: Each, question or incomplete statement is followed by several suggested answers or completions. Select the one that BEST answers the question or completes the statement. *PRINT THE LETTER OF THE CORRECT ANSWER IN THE SPACE AT THE RIGHT.*

1. The determination of a drinking water supply's conformity with established bacteriological requirements is based on   1.____

    A. comparisons with dissolved solids data
    B. correlated oxygen content
    C. average measurement readings of all tests performed
    D. the number of positive tests

2. The magnitude of error associated with a particular data set is known as   2.____

    A. systematic error   B. data quality
    C. standard variance   D. standard error

3. Which type of air quality data report uses a circular figure for presentation, rather than a table or graph?   3.____

    A. Diurnal variation pattern
    B. Pollutant rose
    C. Frequency distribution
    D. Data summarization

4. When the water pressure within a delivery system is greater than the atmospheric pressure, it is called   4.____

    A. gage pressure   B. barometric pressure
    C. vacuum   D. absolute pressure

5. In data evaluation, the term for the variability of measurements of the same quantity gathered using the same method is   5.____

    A. standard deviation   B. precision
    C. accuracy   D. data variability

6. The data used as the PRIMARY criterion for determining the amount of an allowable Industrial waste dump into a flowing stream is   6.____

    A. external climatic factors
    B. projected flow of the watercourse
    C. biotic potential of surrounding waters
    D. toxicity of waste material

7. Once the data have been gathered for an environmental impact assessment, experts play a prominent role in each of the following ways, EXCEPT   7.____

    A. identifying alternatives and control variables
    B. relating input to output variables
    C. gathering more data using techniques of greater refinement
    D. evaluating reliability and applicability of data

8. In determining the quality of a given water sample, concentrations of dissolved elements are expressed in terms of: 8.____

   A. volume   B. mass
   C. particle ratios   D. surface area

9. The errors in a data set that CANNOT be estimated by the use of standard statistical techniques, and usually produce a biased result, are called _____ errors. 9.____

   A. systematic   B. random
   C. clerical   D. standard

10. The method for data presentation MOST commonly used to illustrate the relationship between two sets of continuous data is the 10.____

   A. bar chart   B. histogram
   C. block graph   D. scatter diagram

11. _____ consumption is NOT part of the data set needed to quantitatively evaluate a community's water use. 11.____

   A. Average daily   B. Peak hourly
   C. Peak daily   D. Average hourly

12. The precision of a data set is BEST expressed in terms of 12.____

   A. mode   B. standard deviation
   C. average   D. frequency

13. In water delivery systems, the use of a manometer for measuring water pressure is 13.____

   A. usually limited to indoor, fixed units
   B. a universally adopted practice
   C. most commonly applied to mobile units
   D. seldom used indoors

14. All of the following are problems often associated with the practice of intermittently collecting air quality data EXCEPT 14.____

   A. inaccurate averages
   B. increased likelihood of extreme values
   C. greater meteorological impact on data
   D. increased susceptibility to error

15. Which of the following Is NOT a method used to measure variation within a data set? 15.____

   A. Mean deviation   B. Standard deviation
   C. Range   D. Variance mode

16. The device MOST commonly used to report pipe flow data for a water delivery system is the 16.____

   A. table   B. circular graph
   C. cross-referenced spread sheet   D. nomograph

17. Of the following, the one which is NOT a problem often associated with using the operational gaming model for evaluating environmental impact assessment data is
    A. distancing of interested parties
    B. increased adventurousness of field experts
    C. introduction of human behavioral patterns into the assessment
    D. possibly inaccurate idealization of the system

17.____

18. The chemical analysis of a water sample can be used to determine each of the following factors EXCEPT
    A. dissolved solids   B. alkalinity
    C. biotic potential   D. pH

18.____

19. The air quality data report that groups data according to prevailing wind directions is the
    A. frequency distribution   B. pollutant rose
    C. diurnal variation pattern   D. data summarization

19.____

20. The MOST commonly used device for measuring water pressure in delivery systems is the
    A. piezometer   B. Bourdon gauge
    C. manometer   D. barometric gauge

20.____

21. Each of the following is a problem associated with the use of existing data In making environmental impact assessments EXCEPT the
    A. possibility of different gathering techniques
    B. uncertainty of data accuracy due to time lapse
    C. unsuitabillty of data for an analyst's specific purpose
    D. personal bias of the analyst using the data

21.____

22. The data presentation method that works BEST for illustrating frequency distributions is the
    A. compass graph   B. table
    C. histogram   D. bar graph

22.____

23. The _____ is NOT a factor required in order to calculate storm runoff.
    A. maximum flow rate
    B. area's average rainfall intensity
    C. type and character of runoff surface
    D. minimum flow rate

23.____

24. Which of the characteristics of a data set is almost EXCLUSIVELY involved in the documentation of values, rather than the presentation?
    A. Accuracy   B. Representativeness
    C. Bias   D. Comparability

24.____

25. The MOST frequently appearing value in a data set is known as its
    A. variance standard   B. mode
    C. mid-range   D. median

25.____

KEY (CORRECT ANSWERS)

1.	D	11.	D
2.	B	12.	B
3.	B	13.	A
4.	A	14.	C
5.	B	15.	D
6.	B	16.	D
7.	C	17.	A
8.	B	18.	C
9.	A	19.	B
10.	D	20.	B

21.	D
22.	C
23.	D
24.	A
25.	B

INTERPRETING STATISTICAL DATA GRAPHS, CHARTS AND TABLES

EXAMINATION SECTION
TEST 1

DIRECTIONS: Each question or incomplete statement is followed by several suggested answers or completions. Select the one that BEST answers the question or completes the statement. *PRINT THE LETTER OF THE CORRECT ANSWER IN THE SPACE AT THE RIGHT.*

Questions 1-3.

DIRECTIONS: Questions 1 through 3 are to be answered SOLELY on the basis of the information given below.

Assume that at various hours of a typical day the amounts of chlorine residual in parts per million (ppm) at a certain water treatment plant are as shown in the following graph.

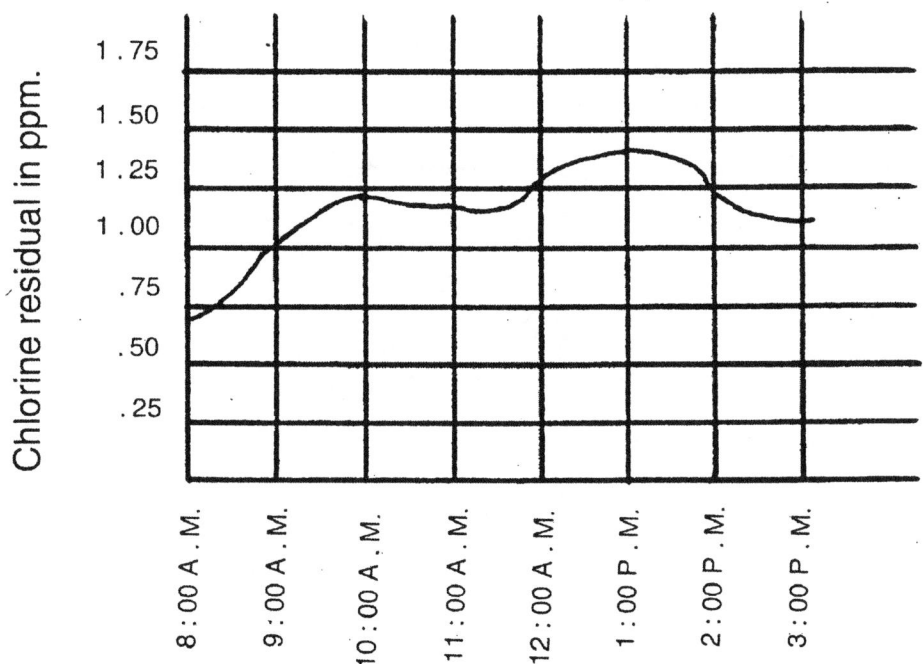

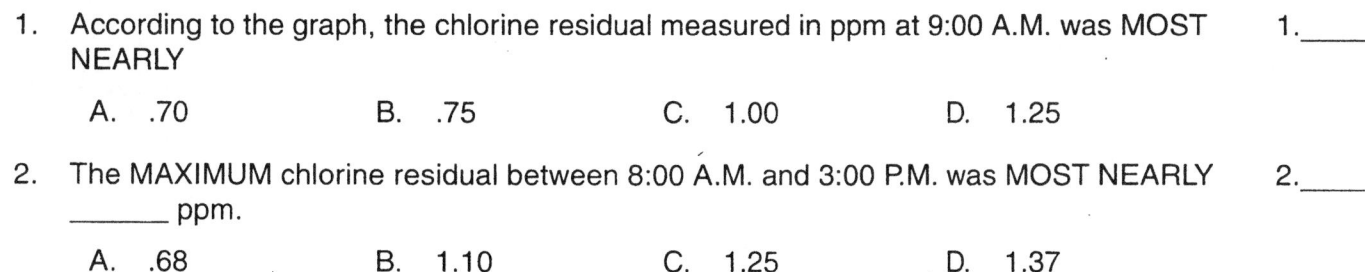

1. According to the graph, the chlorine residual measured in ppm at 9:00 A.M. was MOST NEARLY   1.____

   A. .70   B. .75   C. 1.00   D. 1.25

2. The MAXIMUM chlorine residual between 8:00 A.M. and 3:00 P.M. was MOST NEARLY   2.____
   _____ ppm.

   A. .68   B. 1.10   C. 1.25   D. 1.37

3. According to the graph, between the hours of 12:00 Noon and 1:00 P.M., the chlorine residual was   3.____

    A. always increasing
    B. always decreasing
    C. increasing, then decreasing
    D. decreasing, then increasing

KEY (CORRECT ANSWERS)

    1. C
    2. D
    3. A

TEST 2

Questions 1-3.

DIRECTIONS: Questions 1 through 3 are to be answered SOLELY on the basis of the information given below.
   Assume that a certain water treatment plant has consumed quantities of chemicals E and F over a five-week period, as indicated in the following table.

Time Period	Number of 100-pound sacks consumed	
	Chemical E	Chemical F
Week 1	5	4
Week 2	7	5
Week 3	6	5
Week 4	8	6
Week 5	6	4

1.   The TOTAL number of pounds of Chemical E consumed at the end of the first three weeks is

   A.   180   B.   320   C.   1,400   D.   1,800

2.   According to the table, the week in which the MOST chemicals were consumed was week

   A.   2   B.   3   C.   4   D.   5

3.   According to the table, the AVERAGE number of sacks of Chemical F consumed over the first four weeks was

   A.   4   B.   5   C.   6   D.   7

1.____

2.____

3.____

KEY (CORRECT ANSWERS)

1.   D
2.   C
3.   B

TEST 3

Questions 1-5.

DIRECTIONS: Questions 1 through 5 are to be answered on the basis of the information given in the table below.

Date of Water Meter Reading	Water Meter Readings in Cubic Feet				
	Meter 1	Meter 2	Meter 3	Meter 4	Meter 5
Dec. 31, 2016	12,416	88,990	64,312	26,985	30,057
June 30, 2017	23,094	98,806	71,527	27,336	30,057
Dec. 31, 2017	33,011	07,723	79,292	27,848	30,618
June 30, 2018	42,907	16,915	87,208	28,286	31,247
Dec. 31, 2018	52,603	26,456	95,244	28,742	31,740

NOTE: The maximum readings of each of the above five meters is 99,999 cubic feet. Above that reading, the meters start registering from zero.

NOTE: Assume that the maximum water consumption between consecutive readings is less than 100,000 cubic feet.

1. The meter which showed the LOWEST water consumption for the period June 30, 2018 to December 31, 2018 is Meter

   A. 2   B. 3   C. 4   D. 5

2. The amount of water consumed between June 30, 2017 and December 31, 2017 by the consumers metered by Meter 2 is _____ cubic feet.

   A. 7,723   B. 8,917   C. 91,083   D. 107,723

3. The meter which showed the GREATEST water consumption over the time period December 31, 2016 to December 31, 2018 is Meter

   A. 1   B. 2   C. 3   D. 4

4. The meter which showed EXACTLY the same water consumption for 2018 as in 2017 is Meter

   A. 1   B. 2   C. 4   D. 5

5. The meter which shows EXACTLY TWICE as much water consumption in 2018 as compared to the consumption in 2017 is Meter

   A. 1   B. 3   C. 4   D. 5

1._____
2._____
3._____
4._____
5._____

KEY (CORRECT ANSWERS)

1. C
2. B
3. A
4. B
5. D

TEST 4

Questions 1-3.

DIRECTIONS: Questions 1 through 3 are to be answered ONLY on the basis of the information given below.

At midnight of each day, readings are made of gas consumption meters. Readings for 8 days are as follows:

Sunday	6873 cu.ft.	Thursday	3256 cu.ft.
Monday	8147 cu.ft.	Friday	4962 cu.ft.
Tuesday	0065 cu.ft.	Saturday	6823 cu.ft.
Wednesday	1480 cu.ft.	Sunday	7179 cu.ft.

1. According to the above table, the total gas consumed for the week was MOST NEARLY _____ cubic feet.   1._____

   A. 1,000   B. 4,000   C. 7,000   D. 10,000

2. Gas consumption for Tuesday was MOST NEARLY _____ cubic feet.   2._____

   A. 500   B. 1,000   C. 2,000   D. 8,000

3. The day on which gas consumption was LOWEST was   3._____

   A. Monday   B. Tuesday   C. Wednesday   D. Thursday

KEY (CORRECT ANSWERS)

1. D
2. C
3. A

READING COMPREHENSION
UNDERSTANDING AND INTERPRETING WRITTEN MATERIAL

EXAMINATION SECTION
TEST 1

DIRECTIONS: Each question or incomplete statement is followed by several suggested answers or completions. Select the one that BEST answers the question or completes the statement. *PRINT THE LETTER OF THE CORRECT ANSWER IN THE SPACE AT THE RIGHT.*

Questions 1-5.

DIRECTIONS: Questions 1 through 5 are based on the following passage. You are to answer the questions which follow based SOLELY upon the information in the passage.

More than 700 dolphins and whales piled up on France's Atlantic coast last February and March. Most were common dolphins, but the toll also included striped and bottlenose dolphins — even a few harbor porpoises and fin, beaked, pilot, and minke whales. Many victims had ropes around their tails or had heads or tails cut off; some had been partly butchered for food. To scientists the cause is obvious: These marine mammals were seen as waste, *byaatah,* to the fishermen who snared them in their nets while seeking commercial fish.

Mid-water trawlers are responsible for this, not drift nets, says Anne Collet, a French biologist who examined the carcasses. The European Union has banned large drift nets. Two other European treaties call for bycatch reduction by vessels using huge trawls for hake and other species. But the Bay of Biscay falls beyond the treaties, a painfully obvious loophole.

1. What killed the dolphins and whales at the Bay of Biscay?   1.____

    A. The propellers of recreational motorboats
    B. Fishermen using drift nets to catch commercial fish
    C. Fishermen seeking commercial fish
    D. Fishermen seeking their tails and heads as trophies

2. What is *bycatch?*   2.____

    A. Animals accidentally caught in the same nets used to catch other types of fish
    B. Animals which typically gather close to certain types of fish, allowing fishermen to hunt more than one species at a time
    C. Those parts of animals and fish discarded by fishermen after the catch
    D. Those fish which exceed the fisherman's specified limit and must be thrown back

3. The dolphins and whales were killed around the Bay of Biscay because the   3.____

    A. treaties which protect these species of dolphins and whales do not reach the Bay of Biscay
    B. bodies of the animals were dumped at the Bay of Biscay, but scientists do not know where they were killed
    C. treaties which limit the use of drift nets do not reach the Bay of Biscay
    D. treaties which limit the use of trawls do not reach the Bay of Biscay

4. Where is the Bay of Biscay located?   4._____

    A. France's Pacific coast
    B. France's Atlantic coast
    C. The European Union's Atlantic coast
    D. The French Riviera

5. What types of fish are mid-water trawlers usually used for?   5._____

    A. Common, striped, and bottlenose dolphins
    B. Common dolphins, harbor porpoises, and pilot whales
    C. Hake and pilot, minke, fin, and beaked whales
    D. Hake and other species

Questions 6-10.

DIRECTIONS: Questions 6 through 10 are based on the following passage. You are to
              answer the questions which follow based SOLELY upon the information in the
              passage.

Malaria once infected 9 out of 10 people in North Borneo, now known as Brunei. In 1955, the World Health Organization (WHO) began spraying the island with dieldrin (a DDT relative) to kill malaria-carrying mosquitoes. The program was so successful that the dread disease was virtually eliminated.

Other, unexpected things began to happen, however. The dieldrin also killed other insects, including flies and cockroaches living in houses. At first, the islanders applauded this turn of events, but then small lizards that also lived in the houses died after gorging themselves on dieldrin-contaminated insects. Next, cats began dying after feeding on the lizards. Then, in the absence of cats, rats flourished and overran the villages. Now that the people were threatened by sylvatic plague carried by rat fleas, WHO parachuted healthy cats onto the island to help control the rats.

Then the villagers' roofs began to fall in. The dieldrin had killed wasps and other insects that fed on a type of caterpillar that either avoided or was not affected by the insecticide. With most of its predators eliminated, the caterpillar population exploded, munching its way through its favorite food: the leaves used in thatched roofs.

Ultimately, this episode ended happily: Both malaria and the unexpected effects of the spraying program were brought under control. Nevertheless, the chain of unforeseen events emphasizes the unpredictability of interfering in an ecosystem.

6. The World Health Organization (WHO) began spraying dieldrin on North Borneo in order   6._____
    to

    A. kill the bacteria which causes malaria
    B. kill the mosquitoes that carry malaria
    C. disrupt the foodchain so that malaria-carrying mosquitoes would die
    D. kill the mosquitoes, flies, and cockroaches that carry malaria

7. Which of the following did the dieldrin kill?   7.____

    A. Mosquitoes   B. Rats
    C. Caterpillars   D. All of the above

8. The villagers' roofs caved in because the dieldrin killed   8.____

    A. mosquitoes, flies, rats, and cats
    B. the trees whose leaves are used in thatched roofs
    C. the caterpillar that eats the leaves used in thatched roofs
    D. the predators of the caterpillar that eats the leaves used in thatched roofs

9. Which of the following was NOT a side effect of spraying dieldrin on Borneo?   9.____

    A. Malaria was virtually eliminated.
    B. The rat population exploded.
    C. The cat population exploded.
    D. The caterpillar population exploded.

10. Why did the World Health Organization (WHO) deliver healthy cats to Borneo without try-   10.____
ing to replenish the other animals and insects which had been wiped out by the dieldrin?
The

    A. presence of a healthy cat population was all that was required to restore the balanced ecosystem
    B. rats that cats preyed upon carried an illness threatening to humans
    C. other insects and animals killed by the dieldrin were nuisances and the villagers were happy to be free of them
    D. villagers' had become attached to cats as domestic pets

Questions 11-15.

DIRECTIONS: Questions 11 through 15 are based on the following passage. You are to answer the questions which follow based SOLELY upon the information in the passage.

Historically, towns and cities grew as a natural byproduct of people choosing to live in certain areas for agricultural, business, or recreational reasons. Beginning in the 1920s, private and governmental planners began to think about how an ideal town would be planned. These communities would be completely built before houses were offered for sale. This concept of preplanning, designing, and building an ideal town was not fully developed until the 1960s. By 1976, about forty-three towns could be classified as planned *new towns.*

One example of a new town is Reston, Virginia, located about 40 kilometers west of Washington, D.C. Reston began to accept residents in 1964 and has a projected population of eighty thousand. Because developers tried to preserve the great natural beauty of the area and the high quality of architectural design of its buildings, Reston has attracted much attention. Reston also has innovative programs in education, government, transportation, and recreation. For example, the stores in Reston are within easy walking distance of the residential parts of the community, and there are many open spaces for family activities. Because Reston is not dependent upon the automobile, noise and air pollution have been greatly reduced. Recent research indicates that the residents of Reston have rated their community much higher than residents of less well-planned suburbs.

11. When did the concept of first building a town and then offering houses for sale fully 11.____
develop?

A. 1920s B. 1950s C. 1960s D. 1970s

12. The goal of planners who develop and build ideal towns and suburbs is to 12.____

A. eliminate the tendency of towns and cities to naturally develop around business or recreational centers
B. control population growth
C. regulate the resources devoted to housing and recreation
D. cut down on suburban sprawl by developing communities where residents are not dependent on cars to maintain a high quality of living

13. Which of the following goals did developers have in mind when planning the community 13.____
of Reston?
    I.   Preservation of natural beauty
    II. Communal living spaces
    III. Communal recreational spaces
    IV. High standards of architectural design
The CORRECT answer is:

A. I, II, III, IV   B. I, III, IV
C. II, III, IV   D. I, II, IV

14. The fact that stores in Reston are within easy walking distance of the residential parts of 14.____
the community is an example of innovation in

A. transportation   B. recreation
C. education   D. all of the above

15. What are the environmental advantages to towns like Reston? 15.____

A. Uniform architecture
B. Individual recreational spaces cut down on the overuse of resources
C. Decreased noise and air pollution
D. Ability to control the number and type of residents

Questions 16-20.

DIRECTIONS: Questions 16 through 20 are based on the following passage. You are to answer the questions which follow based SOLELY upon the information in the passage.

Lead is one of the most common toxic (harmful or poisonous) metals in the intercity environment. It is found, to some extent, in all parts of the urban environment (e.g., air, soil, and older pipes and paint) and in all biological systems, including people. There is no apparent biologic need for lead, but it is sufficiently concentrated in the blood and bones of children living in inner cities to cause health and behavior problems. In some populations over *20%* of the children have levels of lead concentrated in their blood above that believed safe. Lead affects nearly every system of the body. Acute lead toxicity may be characterized by a variety of symptoms, including anemia, mental retardation, palsy, coma, seizures, apathy, uncoordination, subtle loss of recently acquired skills, and bizarre behavior. Lead toxicity is particularly a problem for young children who tend to be exposed to higher concentrations in some urban areas and apparently are more susceptible to lead poisoning than are adults. Following exposure to lead and having acute toxic response, some children manifest aggressive, difficult to manage behavior.

The occurrence of lead toxicity or lead poisoning has cultural, political, and sociological implications. Over 2,000 years ago, the Roman Empire produced and used tremendous amounts of lead for a period of several hundred years. Production rates were as high as 55,000 metric tons per year. Romans had a wide variety of uses for lead, including pots in which grapes were crushed and processed into a syrup for making wine, cups, and goblets from which the wine was drunk, as a base for cosmetics and medicines, and finally for the wealthy class of people who had running water in their homes, lead was used to make the pipes that carried the water. It has been argued by some historians that gradual lead poisoning among the upper class in Rome was partly responsible for Rome's eventual fall.

16. In which parts of the urban environment can lead be found?   16._____
      I.   Air
      II. Water
      III. Adults
      IV. Children
    The CORRECT answer is:

    A. I, II, III   B. I, III, IV
    C. II, III, IV   D. All of the above

17. Lead toxicity has the most powerful effect on which of the following?   17._____

    A. Mentally retarded children
    B. Young children
    C. Anemic women
    D. Children who suffer from seizures

18. Romans used lead in which of the following?   18._____

    A. Cosmetics   B. Paint   C. Wine   D. Clothes

19. Humans require a certain level of lead in the bloodstream in order to avoid which of the   19._____
    following?

    A. Anemia
    B. Uncoordination
    C. Seizures
    D. Scientists have found no biological need for lead among humans

20. Which of the following would most directly support the theory that lead poisoning was   20._____
    partially responsible for the fall of Rome?

    A. Evidence of bizarre behavior among ancient Roman leaders
    B. Evidence of lead in the drinking water of ancient Rome
    C. Studies analyzing the lead content of bones of ancient Romans which detect
        increased levels of lead
    D. Evidence of lead in the environment of ancient Rome

Questions 21-25.

DIRECTIONS: Questions 21 through 25 are based on the following passage. You are to answer the questions which follow based SOLELY upon the information in the passage.

The city of Venice, Italy has been known to be slowly sinking, but for a long time no one knew the cause or a solution. Floods were becoming more and more common, especially during the winter storms when the winds drove waters from the Adriatic Sea into the city's streets. Famous for its canals and architectural beauty, Venice was in danger of being destroyed by the very lagoon that had sustained its commerce for more than a thousand years. Then the reason that the city was sinking was discovered: groundwater in the region was being pumped out and used; the depletion of the water table, over time, caused the soil to compress under the weight of the city above it. The wells that influenced Venice, which were located on the Italian mainland as well as on the islands that make up Venice, supplied water to nearly industrial and domestic users.

Once the cause was discovered, the wells were capped .and other sources of water were found; as a result the city has stopped sinking. This is an example of the application of scientific research on the environment to achieve a solution helpful to a major city.

21.   What causes the winter floods in Venice?   21._____

   A.   The disintegration of the canals that used to protect the city from the floods
   B.   Storms that drive waters from the wells into the streets
   C.   The flawed canal system for which the city is famous
   D.   Storms that drive waters from the Adriatic Sea into the streets

22.   Venice was sinking because of depletion of the   22._____

   A.   lagoon upon which the city was founded
   B.   wells used to flood the lagoons
   C.   water table beneath the city
   D.   soil beneath the city

23.   What was the water beneath Venice used for?   23._____

   A.   Wastewater
   B.   To supply water to the famous canals
   C.   To supply drinking water to Venetians
   D.   To supply local industrial users

24.   How was the problem remedied?   24._____

   A.   City leaders regulated use of the wells and found other sources of water.
   B.   The wells were capped.
   C.   Flood water was diverted back to the Adriatic Sea.
   D.   The wells were used to supply water to nearby industrial and domestic users.

25. How were scientists able to restore Venice to its proper (and previous) elevation? 25.____

    A. Venice was not restored to its previous elevation
    B. By diverting water back into the soil beneath Venice
    C. By capping the wells and finding other sources of water
    D. By restoring the water table

——————

KEY (CORRECT ANSWERS)

1.	C	11.	C
2.	A	12.	D
3.	D	13.	B
4.	B	14.	A
5.	D	15.	C
6.	B	16.	D
7.	A	17.	B
8.	D	18.	A
9.	C	19.	D
10.	B	20.	C

21.	D
22.	C
23.	D
24.	B
25.	A

——————

TEST 2

DIRECTIONS: Each question or incomplete statement is followed by several suggested answers or completions. Select the one that BEST answers the question or completes the statement. *PRINT THE LETTER OF THE CORRECT ANSWER IN THE SPACE AT THE RIGHT.*

Questions 1-5.

DIRECTIONS: Questions 1 through 5 are based on the following passage. You are to answer the questions which follow based SOLELY upon the information in the passage.

China, with one-fifth of the world's population, is the most populous country in the world. Between 1980 and 1995, China's population grew by 200 million people — about three-fourths of the population of the United States — to reach 1.2 billion. Although its growth rate is expected to slow somewhat in the coming decades, population experts predict that there will be 1.5 billion Chinese by 2025. But can China's food production continue to keep pace with its growing population? Should China develop a food deficit, it may need to import more grain from other countries than those countries can spare from their own needs.

To give some idea of the potential impact of China on the world's food supply, consider the following examples. All of the grain produced by Norway would be needed to supply two more beers to each person in China. If the Chinese were to eat as much fish as the Japanese do, China would consume the entire world fish catch. Food for all the chickens required for China to reach its goal of 200 eggs per person per year by 2010 will equal all the grain exported by Canada — the world's second largest grain exporter. Increased demand by China for world grain supplies could result in dramatic increases in food prices and precipitate famines in other areas of the world.

1. China's population increased between 1980 and 1995 by

    A. 200 million people
    B. 1.2 billion people
    C. 1.5 billion people
    D. one-fifth of the world's population

1.____

2. If China developed a food deficit, which of the following would most negatively affect the world's supply of food?

    A. Famines resulting from the increased price of grain
    B. Domestic increase in the production of grain to meet the needs of the Chinese people
    C. International increase in the production of grain to meet China's need
    D. Importing more grain from other countries than those countries could spare

2.____

3. Which of the following was a goal the Chinese government hoped to reach by 2010?

    A. Importing Canada's entire supply of grain
    B. Supplying 200 eggs annually to every citizen
    C. A population of 1.5 billion people
    D. Supplying enough fish to each citizen to match Japan's consumption

3.____

4. Which of the following countries exports the most grain?   4.____

    A. China   B. Norway   C. Canada   D. Japan

5. Which of the following groups contains 200 million people?   5.____

    A. The current population of the United States
    B. Three-quarters of the population of the United States
    C. China's current population
    D. Three-quarters of the population of China

Questions 6-10.

DIRECTIONS: Questions 6 through 10 are based on the following passage. You are to answer the questions which follow based SOLELY upon the information in the passage.

On Tuesday, 16 June 1987, the last dusky seaside sparrow *(Ammo-dramus maratimus nigrescens)* died in captivity at Walt Disney World's Discovery Island Zoological Park in Orlando, Florida. The bird was a male that was probably about twelve years old. Originally, this subspecies and several other subspecies were found in the coastal salt marshes on the Atlantic coast of Florida. (A subspecies is a distinct population of a species that has several characteristics that distinguish it from other populations.) One other subspecies, the Smyrna seaside sparrow *(Ammodramus maratimus pelonata)*, is believed to have become extinct several years ago, and a third subspecies, the Cape Sable seaside sparrow *(Ammodramus maratimus mirabilis)*, was listed as an endangered species in 1967. Before the deaths of the last remaining dusky seaside sparrows, a few males were crossed with another subspecies, Scott's seaside sparrow *(Ammodramus maratimus peninsulae)*. Thus, the hybrid offspring between these two subspecies contain some of the genes that made the dusky seaside sparrow unique.

The endangerment and extinction of these different birds was a direct result of the land development and drainage that destroyed the salt-marsh habitat to which they were adapted. The development of Cape Canaveral as a major center for the U.S. space program also resulted in the modification of much of the birds' original habitat and was a partial cause of their extinction.

6. Which of the following subspecies is NOT yet extinct?   6.____

    A. Dusky seaside sparrow
    B. Cape Sable seaside sparrow
    C. Smyrna seaside sparrow
    D. All of the listed subspecies are extinct

7. A subspecies is a population   7.____

    A. within a species that has been crossed with another population within the same species in order to avoid extinction
    B. within a subspecies that has distinguishing characteristics
    C. that has distinguishing characteristics
    D. within a species that has distinguishing characteristics

8. What was the dusky seaside sparrow's natural habitat? 8._____

    A. Coastal salt marshes of Florida
    B. Man-made parks and zoos such as Discovery Land
    C. Flat, desert-like plains around Cape Canaveral
    D. Areas of land development

9. A hybrid is an animal that 9._____

    A. cannot reproduce
    B. is extinct
    C. is the result of a cross between two subspecies
    D. is the result of a cross between two species

10. What caused the extinction of the dusky seaside sparrow? 10._____

    A. An overabundance of predators caused by human influence and development
    B. Destruction of its natural habitat by human development
    C. Inability to reproduce in captivity
    D. All of the above

Questions 11-15.

DIRECTIONS: Questions 11 through 15 are based on the following passage. You are to answer the questions which follow based SOLELY upon the information in the passage.

For more than 600 years only Adelie penguins lived along the chilly shores of the Western Antarctic Peninsula in the Palmer region. Ornithologist and paleontologist Steven Emslie of the University of North Carolina, Wilmington, found Adelie bones in nests near Palmer Station dating from as early as the 14th century.

But two other penguin species have moved in, apparently as the result of a 50-year warming trend that has seen winter temperatures rise seven to nine degrees F and lessened the amount of ice around the peninsula. *Adelies require the edges of pack ice for foraging,* Emslie says. As the ice shrinks, he believes, their numbers decline. Chinstrap penguins, which forage in the open ocean and aren't affected by ice breakup, began to arrive in the 1950s. Gentoos, normally a subantarctic species, first appeared here in 1975. The two newcomers now form a major portion of the region's penguin population.

11. When did new penguin species begin arriving in the Palmer region? 11._____
    A. 1400s   B. 1950s   C. 1975   D. 1990s

12. Which of the following penguin species are NOT affected by ice breakup? 12._____
    A. Adelie   B. Gentoos   C. Chinstrap   D. Emslie

13. What has caused the new penguin species to move into the Palmer region? 13._____

    A. A warming trend
    B. An increase in the amount of pack ice around the peninsula
    C. An increase in the availability of food
    D. All of the above

14. Adelie penguins have lived in the Palmer region since   14.____

    A. the 14th century   B. the early 1900s
    C. the 1950s   D. 1975

15. What effect does the decrease in the amount of pack ice have on Adelie penguins?   15.____

    A. Decreased ability to fight off predators
    B. Increased ability to fight off predators
    C. Increased ability to forage for food
    D. Decreased ability to forage for food

Questions 16-20.

DIRECTIONS: Questions 16 through 20 are based on the following passage. You are to answer the questions which follow based SOLELY upon the information in the passage.

The price of a liter of gasoline is determined by two major factors: (1) the cost of purchasing and processing crude oil into gasoline, and (2) various taxes. Most of the differences in gasoline prices between countries are a result of the differences in taxes and reflect differences in government policy toward motor vehicle transportation.

A major objective of governments is to collect money to build and repair roads, and governments often charge the user by taxing the fuel used by the car or truck. Governments can also discourage the use of automobiles by increasing the cost of fuel. An increase in fuel costs also creates a demand for increased fuel efficiency in all forms of motor transport.

Many European countries raise more money from fuel taxes than they spend on building and repairing roads, while the United States raises approximately 60 percent of the moneys needed for roads from fuel taxes. The relatively low cost of fuel in the United States encourages more travel and increases road repair costs. The cost of taxes to the United States consumer is about 20 percent of the cost of fuel, while in Japan and many European countries, the percentage is 60 to 75 percent.

16. Which of the following is likely to result from an increase in the cost of fuel?   16.____

    A. *Decreased* fuel efficiency
    B. *Increased* fuel efficiency
    C. *Increased* travel
    D. *Increased* road repair costs

17. Which of the following affects the price of gasoline?   17.____

    A. Cost of purchasing crude oil
    B. Cost of processing crude oil
    C. Taxes
    D. All of the above

18. Most governments tax car and truck fuel in order to   18.____

    A. finance the costs of repairing roads
    B. discourage motor travel as much as possible

    C.   finance various social welfare programs
    D.   finance public transportation systems

19.   Differences in _____ accounts for the differences in gasoline prices between countries.   19._____

    A.   the cost of purchasing a car
    B.   the amount of crude oil each country exports
    C.   government taxes
    D.   the number of automobiles imported by individual countries

20.   Which of the following is most likely to discourage travel?   20._____

    A.   *Decrease* in fuel tax
    B.   *Increase* in fuel tax
    C.   *Decrease* in fuel efficiency
    D.   *Increase* in road repair

Questions 21-25.

DIRECTIONS: Questions 21 through 25 are based on the following passage. You are to answer the questions which follow based SOLELY upon the information in the passage.

Wyoming rancher Jack Turnell is one of a new breed of cowpuncher who gets along with environmentalists. He talks about riparian ecology and biodiversity as fluently as he talks about cattle. *I guess I have learned how to bridge the gap between the environmentalists, the bureaucracies, and the ranching industry.*

Turnell grazes cattle on his 32,000-hectare (80,000 acre) ranch south of Cody, Wyoming, and on 16,000 hectares (40,000 acres) of Forest Service land on which he has grazing rights. For the first decade after he took over the ranch, he punched cows the conventional way. Since then, he's made some changes.

Turnell disagrees with the proposals by environmentalists to raise grazing fees and remove sheep and cattle from public rangeland. He believes that if ranchers are kicked off the public range, ranches like his will be sold to developers and chopped up into vacation sites, irreversibly destroying the range for wildlife and livestock alike.

At the same time, he believes that ranches can be operated in more ecologically sustainable ways. To demonstrate this, Turnell began systematically rotating his cows away from the riparian areas, gave up most uses of fertilizers and pesticides, and crossed his Hereford and Angus cows with a French breed that tends to congregate less around water. Most of his ranching decisions are made in consultation with range and wildlife scientists, and changes in range condition are carefully monitored with photographs.

The results have been impressive. Riparian areas on the ranch and Forest Service land are lined with willows and other plant life, providing lush habitat for an expanding population of wildlife, including pronghorn antelope, deer, moose, elk, bear, and mountain lions. And this *eco-rancher* now makes more money because the higher-quality grass puts more meat on his cattle. He frequently talks to other ranchers about sustainable range management; some of them probably think he has been chewing locoweed.

21. The fact that Turnell's decision-making process involves range and wildlife scientists is an example of   21.____

    A. successful government oversight
    B. enforced government regulation
    C. conventional ranching
    D. successful sustainable ranching

22. What is the environmental drawback to removing grazing animals from government range land?   22.____

    A. The loss of ranches which rely on public ranges to real-estate developers
    B. The loss of public range land to real-estate developers
    C. Under-use of public range land
    D. Increased vulnerability to forest fires due to under-use

23. Which of the following is a result of Turnell's decision to rotate his cattle?   23.____

    A. The production of cattle which tend to congregate less around water
    B. Increased bio-diversity which attracts and supports several animal species
    C. The production of beefier, more profitable cattle
    D. All of the above

24. Which of the following is an example of sustainable ranching?   24.____

    A. The use of pesticides to control disease
    B. Non-use of, and non-reliance on, public grazing lands
    C. Rotation of cattle away from riparian areas
    D. Independent decision-making

25. Which of the following is an effect of the increased diversity of plant life on the grazing land that Turnell uses?   25.____

    A. Production of leaner cattle
    B. Production of larger, meatier cattle
    C. Production of more abundant but less nutritious grasses
    D. Less reliance on pesticides

———

KEY (CORRECT ANSWERS)

1.	A		11.	B
2.	D		12.	C
3.	B		13.	A
4.	C		14.	A
5.	B		15.	D
6.	B		16.	B
7.	D		17.	D
8.	A		18.	A
9.	C		19.	C
10.	B		20.	B

21.	D
22.	A
23.	B
24.	C
25.	B

———

PREPARING WRITTEN MATERIAL

PARAGRAPH REARRANGEMENT
COMMENTARY

The sentences which follow are in scrambled order. You are to rearrange them in proper order and indicate the letter choice containing the correct answer at the space at the right.

Each group of sentences in this section is actually a paragraph presented in scrambled order. Each sentence in the group has a place in that paragraph; no sentence is to be left out. You are to read each group of sentences and decide upon the best order in which to put the sentences so as to form as well-organized paragraph.

The questions in this section measure the ability to solve a problem when all the facts relevant to its solution are not given.

More specifically, certain positions of responsibility and authority require the employee to discover connections between events sometimes, apparently, unrelated. In order to do this, the employee will find it necessary to correctly infer that unspecified events have probably occurred or are likely to occur. This ability becomes especially important when action must be taken on incomplete information.

Accordingly, these questions require competitors to choose among several suggested alternatives, each of which presents a different sequential arrangement of the events. Competitors must choose the MOST logical of the suggested sequences.

In order to do so, they may be required to draw on general knowledge to infer missing concepts or events that are essential to sequencing the given events. Competitors should be careful to infer only what is essential to the sequence. The plausibility of the wrong alternatives will always require the inclusion of unlikely events or of additional chains of events which are NOT essential to sequencing the given events.

It's very important to remember that you are looking for the best of the four possible choices, and that the best choice of all may not even be one of the answers you're given to choose from.

There is no one right way to solve these problems. Many people have found it helpful to first write out the order of the sentences, as they would have arranged them, on their scrap paper before looking at the possible answers. If their optimum answer is there, this can save them some time. If it isn't, this method can still give insight into solving the problem. Others find it most helpful to just go through each of the possible choices, contrasting each as they go along. You should use whatever method feels comfortable, and works, for you.

While most of these types of questions are not that difficult, we've added a higher percentage of the difficult type, just to give you more practice. Usually there are only one or two questions on this section that contain such subtle distinctions that you're unable to answer confidently, and you then may find yourself stuck deciding between two possible choices, neither of which you're sure about.

Preparing Written Material

EXAMINATION SECTION
TEST 1

DIRECTIONS: The following groups of sentences need to be arranged in an order that makes sense. Select the letter preceding the sequence that represents the best sentence order. *PRINT THE LETTER OF THE CORRECT ANSWER IN THE SPACE AT THE RIGHT.*

Question 1

1._____

1. The ostrich egg shell's legendary toughness makes it an excellent substitute for certain types of dishes or dinnerware, and in parts of Africa ostrich shells are cut and decorated for use as containers for water.
2. Since prehistoric times, people have used the enormous egg of the ostrich as a part of their diet, a practice which has required much patience and hard work-to hard-boil an ostrich egg takes about four hours.
3. Opening the egg's shell, which is rock hard and nearly an inch thick, requires heavy tools, such as a saw or chisel; from inside, a baby ostrich must use a hornlike projection on its beak as a miniature pick-axe to escape from the egg.
4. The offspring of all higher-order animals originate from single egg cells that are carried by mothers, and most of these eggs are relatively small, often microscopic.
5. The egg of the African ostrich, however, weighs a massive thirty pounds, making it the largest single cell on earth, and a common object of human curiosity and wonder.

The best order is

A. 5 4 1 2 3
B. 1 4 5 3 2
C. 4 2 3 5 1
D. 4 5 2 3 1

Question 2

2._____

1. Typically only a few feet high on the open sea, individual tsunami have been known to circle the entire globe two or three times if their progress is not interrupted, but are not usually dangerous until they approach the shallow water that surrounds land masses.
2. Some of the most terrifying and damaging hazards caused by earthquakes are tsunami, which were once called "tidal waves"— a poorly chosen name, since these waves have nothing to do with tides.
3. Then a wave, slowed by the sudden drag on the lower part of its moving water column, will pile upon itself, sometimes reaching a height of over 100 feet.
4. Tsunami (Japanese for "great harbor wave") are seismic waves that are caused by earthquakes near oceanic trenches, and once triggered, can travel up to 600 miles an hour on the open ocean.
5. A land-shoaling tsunami is capable of extraordinary destruction; some tsunami have deposited large boats miles inland, washed out two-foot-thick seawalls, and scattered locomotive trains over long distances.

The best order is

A. 4 1 3 2 5
B. 1 3 4 2 5
C. 5 1 3 2 4
D. 2 4 1 3 5

Question 3

1. Soon, by the 1940's, jazz was the most popular type of music among American intellectuals and college students.
2. In the early days of jazz, it was considered "lowdown" music, or music that was played only in rough, disreputable bars and taverns.
3. However, jazz didn't take long to develop from early ragtime melodies into more complex, sophisticated forms, such as Charlie Parker's "bebop" style of jazz.
4. After charismatic band leaders such as Duke Ellington and Count Basic brought jazz to a larger audience, and jazz continued to evolve into more complicated forms, white audiences began to accept and even to enjoy the new American art form.
5. Many white Americans, who then dictated the tastes of society, were wary of music that was played almost exclusively in black clubs in the poorer sections of cities and towns.

The best order is

A. 5 4 3 2 1
B. 2 5 3 4 1
C. 4 5 3 1 2
D. 1 2 4 3 5

Question 4

1. Then, hanging in a windless place, the magnetized end of the needle would always point to the south.
2. The needle could then be balanced on the rim of a cup, or the edge of a fingernail, but this balancing act was hard to maintain, and the needle often fell off.
3. Other needles would point to the north, and it was important for any traveler finding his way with a compass to remember which kind of magnetized needle he was carrying.
4. To make some of the earliest compasses in recorded history, ancient Chinese "magicians" would rub a needle with a piece of magnetized iron called a lodestone.
5. A more effective method of keeping the needle free to swing with its magnetic pull was to attach a strand of silk to the center of the needle with a tiny piece of wax.

The best order is

A. 4 2 5 1 3
B. 4 3 5 2 1
C. 4 5 2 1 3
D. 4 1 3 5 2

Question 5

5.____

1. The now-famous first mate of the *HMS Bounty,* Fletcher Christian, founded one of the world's most peculiar civilizations in 1790.
2. The men knew they had just committed a crime for which they could be hanged, so they set sail for Pitcairn, a remote, abandoned island in the far eastern region of the Polynesian archipelago, accompanied by twelve Polynesian women and six men.
3. In a mutiny that has become legendary, Christian and the others forced Captain Bligh into a lifeboat and set him adrift off the coast of Tonga in April of 1789.
4. In early 1790, the *Bounty* landed at Pitcairn Island, where the men lived out the rest of their lives and founded an isolated community which to this day includes direct descendants of Christian and the other crewmen.
5. The *Bounty,* commanded by Captain William Bligh, was in the middle of a global voyage, and Christian and his shipmates had come to the conclusion that Bligh was a reckless madman who would lead them to their deaths unless they took the ship from him.

The best order is

A. 4 5 3 2 1
B. 1 3 5 2 4
C. 1 5 3 2 4
D. 3 1 5 4 2

Question 6

6.____

1. But once the vines had been led to make orchids, the flowers had to be carefully hand-pollinated, because unpollinated orchids usually lasted less than a day, wilting and dropping off the vine before it had even become dark.
2. The Totonac farmers discovered that looping a vine back around once it reached a five-foot height on its host tree would cause the vine to flower.
3. Though they knew how to process the fruit pods and extract vanilla's flavoring agent, the Totonacs also knew that a wild vanilla vine did not produce abundant flowers or fruit.
4. Wild vines climbed along the trunks and canopies of trees, and this constant upward growth diverted most of the vine's energy to making leaves instead of the orchid flowers that, once pollinated, would produce the flavorful pods.
5. Hundreds of years before vanilla became a prized food flavoring in Europe and the Western World, the Totonac Indians of the Mexican Gulf Coast were skilled cultivators of the vanilla vine, whose fruit they literally worshipped as a goddess.

The best order is

A. 2 3 4 1 5
B. 2 4 3 1 5
C. 5 3 4 2 1
D. 3 4 1 2 5

Question 7   7._____

1. Once airborne, the spider is at the mercy of the air currents—usually the spider takes a brief journey, traveling close to the ground, but some have been found in air samples collected as high as 10,000 feet, or been reported landing on ships far out at sea.
2. Once a young spider has hatched, it must leave the environment into which it was born as quickly as possible, in order to avoid competing with its hundreds of brothers and sisters for food.
3. The silk rises into warm air currents, and as soon as the pull feels adequate the spider lets go and drifts up into the air, suspended from the silk strand in the same way that a person might parasail.
4. To help young spiders do this, many species have adapted a practice known as "aerial dispersal," or, in common speech, "ballooning."
5. A spider that wants to leave its surroundings quickly will climb to the top of a grass stem or twig, face into the wind, and aim its back end into the air, releasing a long stream of silk from the glands near the tip of its abdomen.

The best order is

A. 5 4 2 3 1
B. 5 2 4 1 3
C. 2 5 4 3 1
D. 2 4 5 3 1

Question 8   8._____

1. For about a year, Tycho worked at a castle in Prague with a scientist named Johannes Kepler, but their association was cut short by another argument that drove Kepler out of the castle, to later develop, on his own, the theory of planetary orbits.
2. Tycho found life without a nose embarrassing, so he made a new nose for himself out of silver, which reportedly remained glued to his face for the rest of his life.
3. Tycho Brahe, the 17th-century Danish astronomer, is today more famous for his odd and arrogant personality than for any contribution he has made to our knowledge of the stars and planets.
4. Early in his career, as a student at Rostock University, Tycho got into an argument with the another student about who was the better mathematician, and the two became so angry that the argument turned into a sword fight, during which Tycho's nose was sliced off.
5. Later in his life, Tycho's arrogance may have kept him from playing a part in one of the greatest astronomical discoveries in history: the elliptical orbits of the solar system's planets.

The best order is

A. 1 4 2 3 5
B. 4 2 3 5 1
C. 4 2 1 3 5
D. 3 4 2 5 1

Question 9   9._____

1. The processionaries are so used to this routine that if a person picks up the end of a silk line and brings it back to the origin—creating a closed circle—the caterpillars may travel around and around for days, sometimes starving ar freezing, without changing course.
2. Rather than relying on sight or sound, the other caterpillars, who are lined up end-to-end behind the leader, travel to and from their nests by walking on this silk line, and each will reinforce it by laying down its own marking line as it passes over.
3. In order to insure the safety of individuals, the processionary caterpillar nests in a tree with dozens of other caterpillars, and at night, when it is safest, they all leave together in search of food.
4. The processionary caterpillar of the European continent is a perfect illustration of how much some insect species rely on instinct in their daily routines.
5. As they leave their nests, the processionaries form a single-file line behind a leader who spins and lays out a silk line to mark the chosen path.

The best order is

A. 4 3 5 2 1
B. 3 5 4 2 1
C. 3 5 2 1 4
D. 4 5 3 1 2

Question 10   10._____

1. Often, the child is also given a handcrafted walker or push cart, to provide support for its first upright explorations.
2. In traditional Indian families, a child's first steps are celebrated as a ceremonial event, rooted in ancient myth.
3. These carts are often intricately designed to resemble the chariot of Krishna, an important figure in Indian mythology.
4. The sound of these anklet bells is intended to mimic the footsteps of the legendary child Rama, who is celebrated in devotional songs throughout India.
5. When the child's parents see that the child is ready to begin walking, they will fit it with specially designed ankle bracelets, adorned with gently ringing bells.

The best order is

A. 2 3 4 1 5
B. 2 5 3 1 4
C. 5 4 1 3 2
D. 5 3 2 1 4

Question 11

1. The settlers planted Osage orange all across Middle America, and today long lines and
    rectangles of Osage orange trees can still be seen on the prairies, running along the former
    boundaries of farms that no longer exist.
2. After trying sod walls and water-filled ditches with no success, American farmers began to
    look for a plant that was adaptable to prairie weather, and that could be trimmed into a
    hedge that was "pig-tight, horse-high, and bull-strong."
3. The tree, so named because it bore a large (but inedible) fruit the size of an orange, was
    among the sturdiest and hardiest of American trees, and was prized among Native Ameri-
    cans for the strength and flexibility of bows which were made from its wood.
4. The first people to practice agriculture on the American flatlands were faced with an impor-
    tant problem: what would they use to fence their land in a place that was almost entirely
    without trees or rocks?
5. Finally, an Illinois farmer brought the settlers a tree that was native to the land between the
    Red and Arkansas rivers, a tree called the Osage orange.

The best order is

A. 2 1 5 3 4
B. 1 2 3 4 5
C. 4 2 5 3 1
D. 4 2 1 3 5

Question 12

1. After about ten minutes of such spirited and complicated activity, the head dancer is free to
    make up his or her own movements while maintaining the interest of the New Year's crowd.
2. The dancer will then perform a series of leg kicks, while at the same time operating the
    lion's mouth with his own hand and moving the ears and eyes by means of a string which is
    attached to the dancer's own mouth.
3. The most difficult role of this dance belongs to the one who controls the lion's head; this
    person must lead all the other "parts" of the lion through the choreographed segments of
    the dance.
4. The head dancer begins with a complex series of steps, alternately stepping forward with
    the head raised, and then retreating a few steps while lowering the head, a movement that
    is intended to create the impression that the lion is keeping a watchful eye for anything evil.
5. When performing a traditional Chinese New Year's lion dance, several performers must fit
    themselves inside a large lion costume and work together to enact different parts of the
    dance.

The best order is

A. 5 3 4 2 1
B. 3 4 2 5 1
C. 3 1 5 4 2
D. 4 2 3 5 1

Question 13

13.____

1. For many years the shell of the chambered nautilus was treasured in Europe for its beauty and intricacy, but collectors were unaware that they were in possession of the structure that marked a "missing link" in the evolution of marine mollusks.
2. The nautilus, however, evolved a series of enclosed chambers in its shell, and invented a new use for the structure: the shell began to serve as a buoyancy device.
3. Equipped with this new flotation device, the nautilus did not need the single, muscular foot of its predecessors, but instead developed flaps, tentacles, and a gentle form of jet propulsion that transformed it into the first mollusk able to take command of its own destiny and explore a three-dimensional world.
4. By pumping and adjusting air pressure into the chambers, the nautilus could spend the day resting on the bottom, and then rise toward the surface at night in search of food.
5. The nautilus shell looks like a large snail shell, similar to those of its ancestors, who used their shells as protective coverings while they were anchored to the sea floor.

The best order is

A. 5 2 4 1 3
B. 5 1 2 3 4
C. 1 2 5 3 4
D. 1 5 2 4 3

Question 14

14.____

1. While France and England battled for control of the region, the Acadiens prospered on the fertile farmland, which was finally secured by England in 1713.
2. Early in the 17th century, settlers from western France founded a colony called Acadie in what is now the Canadian province of Nova Scotia.
3. At this time, English officials feared the presence of spies among the Acadiens who might be loyal to their French homeland, and the Acadiens were deported to spots along the Atlantic and Caribbean shores of America.
4. The French settlers remained on this land, under English rule, for around forty years, until the beginning of the French and Indian War, another conflict between France and England.
5. As the Acadien refugees drifted toward a final home in southern Louisiana, neighbors shortened their name to "Cadien," and finally "Cajun," the name which the descendants of early Acadiens still call themselves.

The best order is

A. 1 4 2 3 5
B. 2 1 3 5 4
C. 2 1 4 3 5
D. 5 2 3 4 1

Question 15   15.____

1. Traditional households in the Eastern and Western regions of Africa serve two meals a day-one at around noon, and the other in the evening.
2. The starch is then used in the way that Americans might use a spoon, to scoop up a portion of the main dish on the person's plate.
3. The reason for the starch's inclusion in every meal has to do with taste as well as nutrition; African food can be very spicy, and the starch is known to cool the burning effect of the main dish.
4. When serving these meals, the main dish is usually served on individual plates, and the starch is served on a communal plate, from which diners break off a piece of bread or scoop rice or fufu in their fingers.
5. The typical meals usually consist of a thick stew or soup as the main course, and an accompanying starch—either bread, rice, *or fufu, a* starchy grain paste similar in consistency to mashed potatoes.

The best order is

A. 5 2 3 4 1
B. 5 1 4 3 2
C. 1 4 5 3 2
D. 1 5 4 2 3

Question 16   16.____

1. In the early days of the American Midwest, Indiana settlers sometimes came together to hold an event called an apple peeling, where neighboring settlers gathered at the homestead of a host family to help prepare the hosts' apple crop for cooking, canning, and making apple butter.
2. At the beginning of the event, each peeler sat down in front of a ten- or twenty-gallon stone jar and was given a crock of apples and a paring knife.
3. Once a peeler had finished with a crock, another was placed next to him; if the peeler was an unmarried man, he kept a strict count of the number of apples he had peeled, because the winner was allowed to kiss the girl of his choice.
4. The peeling usually ended by 9:30 in the evening, when the neighbors gathered in the host family's parlor for a dance social.
5. The apples were peeled, cored, and quartered, and then placed into the jar.

The best order is

A. 1 5 3 4 2
B. 2 5 3 4 1
C. 1 2 5 3 4
D. 2 1 5 4 3

Question 17   17.____

1.   If your pet turtle is a land turtle and is native to temperate climates, it will stop eating some time in October, which should be your cue to prepare the turtle for hibernation.
2.   The box should then be covered with a wire screen, which will protect the turtle from any rodents or predators that might want to take advantage of a motionless and helpless animal.
3.   When your turtle hasn't eaten for a while and appears ready to hibernate, it should be moved to its winter quarters, most likely a cellar or garage, where the temperature should range between 40° and 45° F.
4.   Instead of feeding the turtle, you should bathe it every day in warm water, to encourage the turtle to empty its intestines in preparation for its long winter sleep.
5.   Here the turtle should be placed in a well-ventilated box whose bottom is covered with a moisture-absorbing layer of clay beads, and then filled three-fourths full with almost dry peat moss or wood chips, into which the turtle will burrow and sleep for several months.

The best order is

A.   1 4 3 5 2
B.   3 4 2 5 1
C.   3 2 4 1 5
D.   4 5 2 3 1

Question 18   18.____

1.   Once he has reached the nest, the hunter uses two sturdy bamboo poles like huge chopsticks to pull the nest away from the mountainside, into a large basket that will be lowered to people waiting below.
2.   The world's largest honeybees colonize the Nepalese mountainsides, building honeycombs as large as a person on sheer rock faces that are often hundreds of feet high.
3.   In the remote mountain country of Nepal, a small band of "honey hunters" carry out a tradition so ancient that 10,000 year-old drawings of the practice have been found in the caves of Nepal.
4.   To harvest the honey and beeswax from these combs, a honey hunter climbs above the nests, lowers a long bamboo-fiber ladder over the cliff, and then climbs down.
5.   Throughout this dangerous practice, the hunter is stung repeatedly, and only the veterans, with skin that has been toughened over the years, are able to return from a hunt without the painful swelling caused by stings.

The best order is

A.   2 4 3 5 1
B.   2 4 1 5 3
C.   5 3 2 4 1
D.   3 2 4 1 5

Question 19   19.____

1. After the Romans left Britain, there were relentless attacks on the islands from the barbarian tribes of northern Germany—the Angles, Saxons, and Jutes.
2. As the empire weakened, Roman soldiers withdrew from Britain, leaving behind a country that continued to practice the Christian religion that had been introduced by the Romans.
3. Early Latin writings tell of a Christian warrior named Arturius (Arthur, in English) who led the British citizens to defeat these barbarian invaders, and brought an extended period of peace to the lands of Britain.
4. Long ago, the British Isles were part of the far-flung Roman Empire that extended across most of Europe and into Africa and Asia.
5. The romantic legend of King Arthur and his knights of the Round Table, one of the most popular and widespread stories of all time, appears to have some foundation in history.

The best order is

A. 5 4 3 2 1
B. 5 4 2 1 3
C. 4 5 2 3 1
D. 4 3 2 1 5

Question 20   20.____

1. The cylinder was allowed to cool until it sould stand on its own, and then it was cut from the tube and split down the side with a single straight cut.
2. Nineteenth-century glassmakers, who had not yet discovered the glazier's modern techniques for making panes of glass, had to create a method for converting their blown glass into flat sheets.
3. The bubble was then pierced at the end to make a hole that opened up while the glassmaker gently spun it, creating a cylinder of glass.
4. Turned on its side and laid on a conveyor belt, the cylinder was strengthened, or tempered, by being heated again and cooled very slowly, eventually flattening out into a single rectangular piece of glass.
5. To do this, the glassmaker dipped the end of a long tube into melted glass and blew into the other end of the tube, creating an expanding bubble of glass.

The best order is

A. 2 5 3 4 1
B. 2 4 5 3 1
C. 3 5 2 4 1
D. 3 1 4 5 2

Question 21   21.____

1.   The splints are almost always hidden, but horses are occasionally born whose splinted
     toes project from the leg on either side, just above the hoof.
2.   The second and fourth toes remained, but shrank to thin splints of bone that fused invisibly
     to the horse's leg bone.
3.   Horses are unique among mammals, having evolved feet that each end in what is essen-
     tially a single toe, capped by a large, sturdy hoof.
4.   Julius Caesar, an emperor of ancient Rome, was said to have owned one of these three-
     toed horses, and considered it so special that he would not permit anyone else to ride it.
5.   Though the horse's earlier ancestors possessed the traditional mammalian set of five toes
     on each foot, the horse has retained only its third toe; its first and fifth toes disappeared
     completely as the horse evolved.

     The best order is

     A.   3 5 2 1 4
     B.   5 3 2 4 1
     C.   3 2 5 1 4
     D.   5 2 3 1 4

Question 22   22.____

1.   The new building materials—some of which are twenty feet long, and weigh nearly six
     tons—were transported to Pohnpei on rafts, and were brought into their present position
     by using hibiscus fiber ropes and leverage to move the stone columns upward along the
     inclined trunks of coconut palm trees.
2.   The ancestors built great fires to heat the stone, and then poured cool seawater on the col-
     umns, which caused the stone to contract and split along natural fracture lines.
3.   The now-abandoned enclave of Nan Madol, a group of 92 man-made islands off the shore
     of the Micronesian island of Pohnpei, is estimated to have been built around the year 500
     A.D.
4.   The islanders say their ancestors quarried stone columns from a nearby island, where
     large basalt columns were formed by the cooling of molten lava.
5.   The structures of Nan Madol are remarkable for the sheer size of some of the stone "logs"
     or columns that were used to create the walls of the offshore community, and today anthro-
     pologists can only rely on the information of existing local people for clues about how Nan
     Madol was built.

     The best order is

     A.   5 4 3 2 1
     B.   5 3 1 4 2
     C.   3 5 4 2 1
     D.   3 1 4 2 5

Question 23   23.____

  1. One of the most easily manipulated substances on earth, glass can be made into ceramic tiles that are composed of over 90% air.

  2. NASA's space shuttles are the first spacecraft ever designed to leave and re-enter the earth's atmosphere while remaining intact.

  3. These ceramic tiles are such effective insulators that when a tile emerges from the oven in which it was fired, it can be held safely in a person's hand by the edges while its interior still glows at a temperature well over 2000° F.

  4. Eventually, the engineers were led to a material that is as old as our most ancient civilizationsglass.

  5. Because the temperature during atmospheric re-entry is so incredibly hot, it took NASA's engineers some time to find a substance capable of protecting the shuttles.

The best order is

    A. 5 2 1 3 4
    B. 2 5 4 1 3
    C. 2 3 1 2 5
    D. 5 4 3 1 2

Question 24   24.____

  1. The secret to teaching any parakeet to talk is patience, and the understanding that when a bird "talks," it is simply imitating what it hears, rather than putting ideas into words.

  2. You should stay just out of sight of the bird and repeat the phrase you want it to learn, for at least fifteen minutes every morning and evening.

  3. It is important to leave the bird without any words of encouragement or farewell; otherwise it might combine stray remarks or phrases, such as "Good night," with the phrase you are trying to teach it.

  4. For this reason, to train your bird to imitate your words you should keep it free of any distractions, especially other noises, while you are giving it "lessons."

  5. After your repetition, you should quietly leave the bird alone for a while, to think over what it has just heard.

The best order is

    A. 1 4 2 5 3
    B. 1 2 4 3 5
    C. 3 2 1 5 4
    D. 3 1 5 4 2

Question 25   25.____

1. As a school approaches, fishermen from neighboring communities join their fishing boats together as a fleet, and string their gill nets together to make a huge fence that is held up by cork floats.
2. At a signal from the party leaders, or *nakura,* the family members pound the sides of the boats or beat the water with long poles, creating a sudden and deafening noise.
3. The fishermen work together to drag the trap into a half-circle that may reach 300 yards in diameter, and then the families move their boats to form the other half of the circle around the school of fish.
4. The school of fish flee from the commotion into the awaiting trap, where a final wall of net is thrown over the open end of the half-circle, securing the day's haul.
5. Indonesian people from the area around the Sulu islands live on the sea, in floating villages made of lashed-together or stilted homes, and make much of their living by fishing their home waters for migrating schools of snapper, scad, and other fish.

The best order is

A. 1 5 3 4 2
B. 1 2 4 3 5
C. 5 1 2 3 4
D. 5 1 3 2 4

———

KEY (CORRECT ANSWERS)

1.	D	11.	C
2.	D	12.	A
3.	B	13.	D
4.	A	14.	C
5.	C	15.	D
6.	C	16.	C
7.	D	17.	A
8.	D	18.	D
9.	A	19.	B
10.	B	20.	A

21. A
22. C
23. B
24. A
25. D

———

Preparing Written Material

EXAMINATION SECTION
TEST 1

DIRECTIONS: Each short paragraph below is followed by four restatements or summaries of the information contained within it. Select the one that most completely and accurately restates the information or opinion given in the paragraph. *PRINT THE LETTER OF THE CORRECT ANSWER IN THE SPACE AT THE RIGHT*

1. Australia's koalas live solely on a diet of the leaves of the eucalyptus tree, a low-protein food that requires a koala to eat about three or four pounds of leaves a day. For most mammals, these strong-smelling leaves, saturated with toxins such as phenols and the oily compound known as cineole, are among the least digestible foods on the planet. However, the koala is equipped with a digestive system that is able to handle these toxins, trapping the tiniest leaf particles for as much as eight days while the sugars, proteins, and fats are extracted.

    1.____

    A. Because eucalyptus leaves contain a large amount of toxins and oils, it takes a long time for koalas to digest them.
    B. Koalas have to eat three or four pounds of eucalyptus leaves a day, because the leaves are so poor in nutrients.
    C. Koalas have a unique digestive system that allows them to exist solely on a diet of eucalyptus leaves, which are generally toxic and inedible.
    D. The digestive system of the koala illustrates the unique evolutionary palette of the Australian continent.

2. Norway's special geopolitical position - it was the only NATO country to share a border with Russia - drove it to adopt much more cautious policies than other European countries during the Cold War. Its decision to join NATO led to strong protests from Russia, and in order to avoid provocation, Norway's foreign policy had to balance the need for ensuring defense capability with the need to keep tensions at the lowest possible level. Norway's low-tension "base policy" made clear the nation's refusal to allow foreign military forces on Norwegian territory as long as the country is not attacked or threatened with an attack.

    2.____

    A. Norway's "base policy," in spite of its shared border with Russia, is the work of a pacifist nation that should serve as a model for foreign diplomacy everywhere.
    B. When Norway joined NATO, Russia feared a ground invasion over their shared border.
    C. The "base policy" of Norway is a perfect illustration of how much of Europe during the Cold War was a powder keg ready to explode at the slightest provocation.
    D. As the only member of the NATO alliance to border on Russia, Norway was forced to adopt a more conciliatory foreign policy than other members of the alliance.

3. During the women's suffrage movement of the early twentieth century, it was typical of   3.____
   many psychologists and anti-suffragists to automatically associate feminism with mental
   illness. In 1918, H. W. Frink wrote of feminists: "A certain proportion of at least the most
   militant suffragists are neurotics who in some instances are compensating for masculine
   trends, in others, are more or less successfully sublimating sadistic and homosexual
   ones." In the United States, anti-suffragists, finding comfort in psychology, concluded that
   suffragists all bordered hysteria and, thus, their arguments could not be taken seriously.

   A. The relationship between suffragism and feminism led many scientists to conclude
      that suffragists were afflicted with some kind of mental illness.
   B. During the women's suffrage movement, anti-suffragists such as H.W. Frink tended
      to label women who fought for voting rights as mentally ill in order to dismiss their
      arguments.
   C. Responses to the women's suffrage movement are indicative of the tendency to
      label those who challenge the status quo as "Crazy" than to confront their argu-
      ments.
   D. Most of the women who fought for suffrage during the early twentieth century were
      feminists who were mentally ill.

4. All of the earth's early plant life lived in the ocean, and most of these plants were concen-   4.____
   trated in the shallow coastal waters, where the sun's energy could be easily absorbed.
   Because of the constant advance and retreat of tides in these regions, the plantsmostly
   algaewere repeatedly exposed to the atmosphere, and were forced to adapt to life out of
   water. It took millions of years before plant species had evolved that could survive out of
   the sea altogether, with stems that drew water from the ground, and a waxy covering to
   keep them from drying in the sun.

   A. After spending millions of years underwater, the earth's plants finally evolved ways
      of surviving on land.
   B. Most algaes today, because of evolutionary advances, are able to survive for
      extended periods of time out of water.
   C. Despite the fact that plants began as purely underwater organisms, they have
      always needed the sun's energy to survive.
   D. Land plants evolved from sea plants after millions of years in response to the grad-
      ual warming of the earth's atmosphere.

5. Because of the unique convergence of mild temperatures and abundant rain (17 feet a   5.____
   year), British Columbia's temperate coastal rainforest is the most biologically productive
   ecosystem on earth. It's also an increasingly rare and vulnerable ecosystem: in its
   Holocene heyday, it covered only 0.2 percent of the earth's land surface. Today, logging
   and other development have consumed more than half this original range.

   A. The uniquely productive ecosystem of British Columbia's coastal rainforest has
      always been small, and has been reduced by human activity.
   B. Despite the fact that it is the most biologically productive ecosystem on earth, the
      coastal rainforest of British Columbia has been largely ignored by environmental
      activists.
   C. The coastal rainforests of British Columbia have been nearly devastated by logging
      and other development.
   D. British Columbia's coastal rainforest originated during the Holocene Era, but has
      declined steadily ever since.

6. The Roman Empire, which ruled much of the Western world for hundreds of years, was led by an aristocratic class famous for its tendency to drink large amounts of wine. Recently, an American medical researcher theorized that this taste for wine was eventually what caused the decline and fall of the empirenot the drinking of the wine itself, but a gradual poisoning from the lead that was used to line and seal Roman wine casks. The researcher, Dr. S.C. Gilfillan, argues that this lead poisoning specifically affected members of the Empire's ruling class, because they were the Romans most likely to consume wine and other products, like preserved fruits, that were stored in lead-lined jars.

6._____

   A. The Roman aristocracy's taste for wine and dried fruits, according to one researcher, is a cautionary tale about the consequences of overindulgence.
   B. While the Roman Empire's ruling class suffered from widespread lead poisoning, most commoners remained in good health throughout the empire.
   C. One of the most far-fetched theories about the fall of the Roman Empire concerns itself with the lead used to line the wine casks and fruit jars of the ruling class.
   D. An American medical researcher has theorized that the fall of the Roman Empire was caused by slow poisoning from the lead used to line and seal Roman wine casks and fruit jars.

7. In the second century B.C., King Hiero of Syracuse called upon the renowned scientist, Archimedes, to find a way to see if his crown was made of pure gold or a combination of metals. Archimedes came upon the solution some time later, as he was entering a tub full of hot water and noticed that the weight of his body displaced a certain amount of water. Realizing that this same principle could be used on the crown, he forgot himself with excitement, jumping out of the tub and running naked through the town, yelling "Eureka! Eureka!"

7._____

   A. Archimedes, in making his famous discovery, unknowingly contributed the work "Eureka" to the English vocabulary.
   B. The relative purity of gold can be determined by the amount of water it displaces when submerged.
   C. Archimedes, after discovering the solution to a scientific problem while stepping into his tub, became so excited that he ran through the town naked.
   D. The word "Eureka" has become a part of the English language because of an interesting story involving the ancient scientist, Archimedes.

8. In the nineteenth century most Americans had never heard of, let alone tasted, an abalone, the marine mollusk considered to be a delicacy by many Asians, and undisturbed abalone populations thrived all along the west coast. When the California Gold Rush of the 1840s and 1850s brought thousands of Asian immigrants to America, many of these people began to harvest the dense beds of abalone that inhabited the state's intertidal zone. The Asian harvests eventually brought in annual catches of over 4 million pounds of abalone, and as a result, some county governments passed ordinances making it illegal to dive for abalone in waters less than twenty feet deep.

8._____

   A. The Asians who immigrated to California during the Gold Rush harvested so much abalone from intertidal waters that some governments were compelled to limit abalone diving.
   B. Abalone diving was unheard of in California before the Gold Rush, when many Asians immigrated to the state and began to harvest abalone from the intertidal zone.

C. The extreme shortage of abalone in California's intertidal waters can be traced to the Asians who immigrated during the Gold Rush.

D. The abalone of California's coastal waters generally live in waters less than twenty feet deep, where they are now protected by most county governments.

9. Maria Tallchief, the daughter of a full-blood Osage Indian from Oklahoma, was America's first internationally celebrated prima ballerina, rising to stardom at a time when classical American ballet was still struggling to gain international acceptance and acclaim. Her innovative interpretations of such classics as "Swan Lake" and "The Nutcracker" helped convince critics worldwide that American ballet was a force to be reckoned with, and her glamorous beauty helped popularize ballet in America at a time when very few people took it seriously

    9._____

A. As ballet grew more popular in America, Maria Tallchief became a phenomenon in Europe, helping to secure a worldwide reputation for excellence for American ballet.

B. Nobody in American took ballet seriously until the beautiful Maria Tallchief became an international star.

C. With her beauty and technical innovations, Maria Tallchief gained unprecedented critical and popular success for American ballet.

D. Before the success of Maria Tallchief, there were not many ballet dancers in the United States worth noticing.

10. Early in the Constitutional Convention of 1787, the idea of a two-tiered legislature was agreed upon by the framers of the Constitution. The final form of each of the resulting houses, however, was an issue that was debated openly, and which was finally resolved by the "great compromise" of the Constitutional Convention. While the House of Representatives was intended to be a large, politically sensitive body, the Senate was designed to be a moderating influence that would check the powers of the House.

    10._____

A. The framers of the Constitution could not agree on whether the nation's legislature should be bicameral, or two-tiered, at first, but after the "great compromise," they devised a House and Senate.

B. The Constitutional Convention of 1787 ended with the "great compromise" that gave the nation its two-tiered legislature.

C. After much behind-the-scenes dealmaking, the two-tiered legislature of the United States was devised by the framers of the Constitution.

D. The framers of the Constitution, after some debate, decided on a two-tiered legislature made up of a House of Representatives and a Senate that was less susceptible to regional politics.

11. Although scientists have succeeded in creating robots able to process huge amounts of information, they are still struggling to create one whose reasoning ability matches that of a human baby. The main challenge facing these scientists is the difficulty of understanding and imitating the complex process of human perception and reasoning, which involve the ability to register and analyze even the smallest changes in the external environment, and then to act on those changes.

    11._____

A. Even the most sophisticated robot is unable to imitate innate human abilities such as learning to walk, converse or perceive depth.

B. Because of their inability to process large amounts of information, robots have yet to achieve even the most fundamental level of reasoning

C. Despite considerable technological advances, scientists have as yet been unable to produce a robot that can respond intelligently to changes in its environment.
D. Because robots cannot automatically filter out all extraneous information and focus on the most important details of a given situation, they are unable to reason as well as humans.

12. Thor Heyerdahl, a Norwegian anthropologist, had long held the opinion that the Polynesian inhabitants of South Pacific islands such as Samoa, Tonga, and Fiji had actually been migrants from South America. To prove that this was possible, in 1947 Heyerdahl made a crude raft out of balsa wood, which he named after an Incan sun god, *Kon-Tiki,* and sailed from the coast of Peru to the islands east of Tahiti.   12.____

    A. Thor Heyerdahl's 1947 voyage on the *Kon-Tiki* proved that Polynesians probably had common ancestors in South America.
    B. While Thor Heyerdahl's Kon-Tiki voyage suggested a South American origin for Polynesians, most experts today believe the great migrations were launched from somewhere near Indonesia.
    C. To support the idea that Polynesians could have sailed from South America to the Pacific Islands, Thor Heyerdahl sailed the *Kon-Tiki* from Peru to Tahiti in 1947.
    D. Thor Heyerdahl's famous raft, the *Kon-Tiki,* was named for an Incan sun god, and was so well-made that it made it from Peru to Tahiti.

13. During the Age of Exploration, after thousands of miles of open sea, ships entered the bays of the Azore Islands, west of Portugal, with tattered sails, battered hulls, crewmen weakened from scurvyand cargo holds laden with the treasure they had gained on their long trading journeys. Spanish, English and Dutch warships prowled the waters around the Azores to protect this treasure, sometimes even sinking their own ships to keep it from falling into enemy hands. During these fierce battles, many ships filled with treasure were sent to the ocean floor, where they still remain, preserved by the cold saltwater and centuries of rest.   13.____

    A. Although they are now sparsely populated, the Azore Islands were once a resting place for every ship returning from a long journey to the Americas.
    B. Many treasure hunters and archaeologists believe the sea floor around the Azores, a group of islands west of Portugal, still harbors some of the richest sunken treasure in the world.
    C. Economic competition between the European powers was so intense during the Age of Exploration that captains would rather sink their own ships rather than let their treasure fall into enemy hands.
    D. The rich history of the Azore Islands has deposited a large amount of sunken treasure in their surrounding waters.

14. The Whigs, a short-lived American political party. were wary of a domineering president, and many of them believed that the legislative branch should govern the nation. In particular, Whig leader Henry Clay often attempted to bully and belittle President John Tyler into submission. Tyler's resistance to Clay's high-handed tactics strengthened the office of the presidency, and in particular gave greater credibility to all later vice presidents who happened to succeed to the office.   14.____

A.   While U.S. politics was at first dominated by the legislature, President John Tyler shifted the center of power to the presidency, while laying the groundwork for the downfall of the Whig Party.
B.   President John Tyler, a failure by almost any other measure, can at least be credited with contributing to the strength of the presidency.
C.   Henry Clay, who believed in a strong legislature, failed to win much influence over presidents who were not from the Whig Party.
D.   President John Tyler, in resisting Henry Clay's bullying tactics, strengthened the U.S. presidency and lent credibility to the authority of vice presidential successors to the presidency.

15. By far the richest city on earth, Tokyo, Japan is also one of the most overcrowded; most of its people are only able to afford living in extremely small houses and apartments. In addition to cramped housing, Tokyo's overpopulation has created a commuter problem so grim that a corps of "pushers" has been hired by the city, to stand outside crowded commuter trains and help pack people inside. Problems such as these are so severe in Tokyo that there has been serious talk in recent years of moving Japan's capital elsewhere.   15._____

A.   Despite the example of Tokyo, there is no evidence to suggest that economic wealth and overpopulation are related variables.
B.   Tokyo's prosperity has led to such overcrowding that the country of Japan has recently begun to consider moving its capital to another location.
C.   Despite being the richest city on earth, Tokyo, Japan is seriously overcrowded.
D.   The small houses and apartments of Tokyo, along with it overcrowded transit system, are a perfect example of how economic wealth does not always improve a society's quality of life.

16. One of the greatest, and least publicized, legacies of Native American culture has been the worldwide cultivation of food staples through careful farming methods. Over centuries, tribes throughout North and South America domesticated the wild plants that have come to produce over half of the vegetables the world eats today. Corn, or maize, was first cultivated in the Mexican highlands almost seven thousand years ago, from a common wild grass called teosinte, and both potatoes and tomatoes were originally domesticated by the Peruvian Incas from native plants that still grow throughout Peru and Bolivia.   16._____

A.   Explorers of the Americas carried many native vegetables back to Europe, where they continued to adapt and flourish over the centuries.
B.   Today's common corn is a descendant of the wild Mexican teosinte plant, and potatoes and tomatoes were originally grown by the Incas.
C.   Without the agricultural knowledge and skill of early Native Americans, much of the world today would be in danger of famine.
D.   Foods that are today grown and eaten almost worldwide, such as corn, tomatoes, and potatoes, were first cultivated by the natives of North and South

17. America's transportation sector-95 percent of it driven by oil-consumes two-thirds of the petroleum used in the United States. With the 400 million cars now on the world's roads expected to grow to 1 billion by the year 2020, oil-foreign or not-and other finite fossil-fuel resources will some day be conversation pieces for the nostalgic, rather than components of the nation's energy mix.   17._____

A. In the future, most motor vehicles in the United States will be powered by an alternative energy source such as hydrogen or solar power.
B. The continued growth of the oil-dependent transportation sector is outpacing the capacity of fossil-fuel energy resources.
C. Our nation's dependence on foreign oil is a serious vulnerability that can only be corrected by increased domestic production.
D. In the future, 1 billion cars across the world will be competing for oil and gasoline.

18. Althea Gibson, the first African American to win the Wimbledon Tennis Championship,   18.____
began her career by riding the subway out of her neighborhood in Harlem to 143rd Street, where she played paddle tennis against anyone who dared to challenge her. Since the Wimbledon tournament was played on grass, Gibson knew she would have to prepare herself by training on a surface that returned balls as quickly as a grass court. She found the solution to this problem in the gyms of Harlem, whose wood floors allowed her to perfect the rapid volley that helped her win two Wimbledon championships.

A. Althea Gibson's tennis skills, including her famous volley, were developed in and around the inner-city neighborhood of Harlem.
B. Althea Gibson had to leave her neighborhood to learn tennis, but to perfect her game, she had to return home to Harlem.
C. Without the wood floors in the gyms of her Harlem neighborhood, Althea Gibson probably wouldn't have developed a volley that would help her win two Wimbledon tennis championships.
D. Although Althea Gibson achieved international fame as the first African-American to win the Wimbledon Tennis Championship, the path she followed to that championship was as unorthodox as the champion herself.

19. The greenhouse effect is a naturally occurring process that aids in heating the Earth's   19.____
surface and atmosphere. It results from the fact that certain atmospheric gases, such as carbon dioxide, water vapor, and methane, are able to change the energy balance of the planet by being able to absorb longwave radiation from the Earth's surface. Without the greenhouse effect, life on this planet would probably not exist, as the average temperature of the Earth would be a chilly 5 degrees, rather than the present 59 degrees.

A. The naturally-occurring greenhouse effect, by which atmospheric air is warmed, enables life to exist on earth.
B. The greenhouse effect is a completely natural phenomenon that has nothing to do with human activity, and in fact it is beneficial to the planet's ecosystems.
C. Human contributions to the increases in the greenhouse effect threaten life on earth.
D. In order for life to exist on earth, there must be some kind of greenhouse effect.

20. The religious and scientific communities have for centuries been at odds with each other,   20.____
and held opposing viewpoints concerning the origin and nature of life. Progressive thinkers from both groups, however, claim that the two communities, in their ways of seeking answers to humanity's most important questions, share a common set of goals and procedures that would benefit greatly from a cooperative effort.

A. Scientists and theologists will probably never agree on the origin and nature of life, though some progressive thinkers are trying to change the way the two communities talk about these issues.
B. Though most scientists do not believe in God, progressive religious thinkers are continually trying to persuade them otherwise.
C. Progressive religious and scientific thinkers have identified shared goals and questions that the two communities can work together to achieve and solve.
D. Religious thinkers, who usually scorn such scientific theories as evolution, have begun to acknowledge the usefulness of science in answering important questions.

21. The administrations of Presidents Richard Nixon and Jimmy Carter oversaw an Export-Import Bank that was increasingly active in trade promotion, with expanding programs and lending authority. During this period, expenditures for program activities expanded to five times their 1969 rate, but the bank's net income dropped sharply-the low interest rates at which the bank financed its loan programs were lowering its profits.

21.____

A. During the Nixon and Carter administrations, the budget of the Export-Import Bank grew to five times its 1969 expenditures.
B. Though the Export-Import Bank was very active during the Nixon and Carter administrations, its profits were reduced by its low interest rates.
C. Both the Nixon and Carter administrations demonstrated a lack of fiscal discipline that led to a declining net income at the Export-Import Bank.
D. Presidents Nixon and Carter both favored an activist Export-Import Bank, but while Nixon emphasized the function of trade promotion, Carter was more focused on making loans.

22. The Kombai and Korawai tribes of eastern Indonesia are known as the "tree people" for their custom of living in large tree houses, built as high as 150 feet above ground to avoid attacks from their enemies. These houses are built mostly from the fronds of the sago palm, a plant that also serves to produce one of the tree people's primary food sources-the larvae, or grub, of the scarab beetle. The tree people cultivate grubs by cutting a stretch of sago forest and then, after splitting and tying the palms together, leaving the palms to rot.

22.____

A. The food-gathering methods of the Kombai and Korawai illustrate that deforestation is not a contemporary problem.
B. The Kombai and Korawai people of eastern Indonesia rely on the sago palm for both food and housing.
C. The Kombai and Korawai fears of enemy attacks have led them to build their trees high in the forest canopy.
D. Among the world's least-tamed native cultures are the Kombai and Korawai of Irian Jaya, the easternmost region of Indonesia.

23. It's no secret that corporate and federal information networks continue to deal with increasing bandwidth needs. The appetite for datawhether it's for Internet access, file delivery, or the integration of digital voice applicationsisn't likely to level off any time soon, and most information technology professionals allow that there is cause for concern. But emerging technologies for increasing raw bandwidth, accompanied by the streamlining and maturing of transfer and switching protocols, are a good bet to accommodate the hunger for bandwidth, at least into the near future.

23.____

A. There are two ways to decrease the demand for more bandwidth over computer networks: either increase the "raw" amount of bandwidth available over an infra-structure, or devise more efficient transfer and switching protocols.
B. Emerging technologies, aimed at the constantly increasing demand for bandwidth, are some day likely to result in virtually unlimited bandwidth for computer networks.
C. Man different applications contribute to the demand for bandwidth over a computer network, and so the technologies that are devised to meet this demand must be many-faceted.
D. While there is always a need for more bandwidth on large computer networks, newer technologies promise to increase the supply in the near term.

24. In the year 805, a Japanese Buddhist monk named Dengyo Daishi returned from his studies in China with some tea seeds, which he planted on a Japanese mountainside. In China, tea had long been the favorite drink of monks, because it helped them stay awake and attentive during their long periods of meditation, and Dengyo Daishi wanted to bring this practice to Japan. Over the centuries, tea-drinking would prove to be a custom that would influence nearly every aspect of Japanese culture, and Dengyo Daishi has long been considered a sort of saint among the Japanese.   24._____

   A. Because of the cultural similarities between China and Japan, it was only a matter of time before the ritual of tea-drinking made its way from the mainland to the island empire.
   B. Dengyo Daishi, the first person to plant tea seeds in Japan, is revered among today's Japanese.
   C. The Japanese tea-drinking custom was begun in 805 by a Buddhist monk who brought tea seeds from China.
   D. Without the shared cultural traditions of Buddhism, it is unlikely that tea ever would have been imported from China to Japan.

25. Aztec women held a position in society that was far more respected than that of women in most Western civilizations of the time. For example, an Aztec wife was free to divorce a man who failed to provide for their children, or who was physically abusive, and once divorced, a woman was free to remarry whomever she chose. Perhaps the unusually high regard for Aztec women is best illustrated by the traditional Aztec religious belief that a special, elevated status in the afterlife was reserved for only two types of Aztec cit-izens-warriors who had died defending their tribe, and women who had died during child-birth.   25._____

   A. The rights and privileges of Aztec women demonstrate that they were more respected by their societies than women of many cultures of the time.
   B. In the Aztec culture, women had the same rights and status as the most exalted men.
   C. Though the rights of Aztec women were still generally inferior to those of men, most Aztec women were granted a high degree of independence due to their ser-vice to the community.
   D. The relatively high position that Aztec women held in their society reveals the Aztec culture to be well ahead of its time.

KEY (CORRECT ANSWERS)

1.	C		11.	C
2.	D		12.	C
3.	B		13.	D
4.	A		14.	D
5.	A		15.	B
6.	D		16.	D
7.	C		17.	B
8.	A		18.	A
9.	C		19.	A
10.	D		20.	C

21. B
22. B
23. D
24. C
25. A

ARITHMETICAL REASONING
EXAMINATION SECTION
TEST 1

DIRECTIONS: Each question or incomplete statement is followed by several suggested answers or completions. Select the one that BEST answers the question or completes the statement. *PRINT THE LETTER OF THE CORRECT ANSWER IN THE SPACE AT THE RIGHT.*

1. The population of a city is, approximately, 7.85 million. The area is approximately 200 square miles. The number of thousand persons per square mile is
   A. 3.925   B. 39.25   C. 392.5   D. 39250

   1.____

2. The longest straight line that can be drawn to connect two points on the circumference of a circle whose radius is 9 inches is
   A. 9 inches   B. 18 inches   C. 28.2753 inches   D. 4.5 inches

   2.____

3. It is believed that every even number is the sum of two prime numbers. Two prime numbers whose sum is 32 are
   A. 7, 25   B. 22, 21   C. 13, 19   D. 17, 15

   3.____

4. To divide a number by 3000, we should *move* the decimal point 3 places to the
   A. right and divide by 3   B. left and divide by 3
   C. right and multiply by 3   D. left and multiply by 3

   4.____

5. The difference between the area of a rectangle 6 ft. by 4 ft. and the area of a square having the *same* perimeter is
   A. 1 sq. ft.   B. 2 sq. ft.   C. 4 sq. ft.   D. none of these

   5.____

6. The ratio of 1/4 to 3/8 is the *same* as the ratio of
   A. 1 to 3   B. 2 to 3   C. 3 to 2   D. 3 to 4

   6.____

7. If 7½ is divided by 1 1/5, the quotient is
   A. 6 1/4   B. 9   C. 7 1/10   D. 6 3/5

   7.____

8. A farmer has a cylindrical metal tank for watering his stock. It is 10 ft. in diameter and 3 ft. deep. If one cubic foot contains about 7.5 gallons, the *approximate* capacity of the tank in gallons is
   A. 12   B. 225   C. 4   D. 1707

   8.____

9. The fraction which fits in the following series, 1/2, 1/10, _____, 1/250, is
   A. 1/20   B. 1/100   C. 1/10   D. 1/50

   9.____

10. In two years, $200 with interest compounded semi-annually at 4% will amount to
    A. $216.48   B. $233.92   C. $208   D. $216

    10.____

SOLUTIONS TO ARITHMETICAL REASONING

1. Answer: (B) 39.25

   $$200\overline{)8,000,000}\frac{40,000}{}$$ (number of persons per square mile) (approximate population)

   Answer: 39.25 or (approximately) 40 (thousand persons per sq. mi.)

2. Answer: (B) 18 inches

   9" + 9" = 18 inches

3. Answer: (C) 13, 19

   A prime number is an integer which cannot be divided except by itself and one integer; a whole number as opposed to a fraction or a decimal.

4. Answer: (B) 3 places to the left and divide by

   $$3\overline{)6.000.}^{2}$$

5. Answer: (A) 1 sq. ft.

   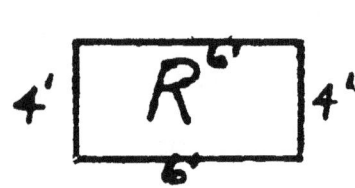

   P = 20 ft.
   A = 24 sq. ft.

   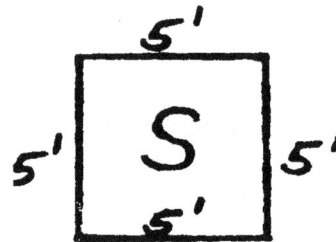

   P = 20 ft.
   A = 25 sq. ft.

   25 − 24 = 1

6. Answer: (B) 2 to 3

   $$\frac{1/4}{3/8}=1/4\div3/8=1/4\times3/8=2/3$$

7. Answer: (A) 6 1/4

   $$\frac{7\,1/2}{1\,1/2}=\frac{15}{2}\div\frac{6}{5}=\frac{15}{2}\times\frac{5}{6}=\frac{25}{4}=6\frac{1}{4}\quad\text{OR}\quad 1.2\overline{)7.5}6\frac{3}{12}\frac{1}{4}$$

1.____
2.____
3.____
4.____
5.____
6.____
7.____

8.   Answer: (B) 225

   $A = irR^2$
   $\quad = 3(5)^2$
   $\quad = 75$ sq. ft.

   225
   ×7.5
   1125

   1575   gal
   1687.5

Volume of tank = 75 × 3 = 225 cu. ft.
(approximate capacity of tank in gallons)

9.   Answer: (D) 1/50
   A geometric series: each number is multiplied by the same number to get the suc-
   ceeding number. (Multiply each number by 1/5). ½, 1/10, 1/50/$216, 1/250. The
   missing number if 1/50.

10   Answer: (A) $216.48
   Compound Interest
   4% a year compounded semi-annually is the same as 2% for a half year

   A. $200 $200
      ×.02   × 4
      $4.00 Interest for 1st half yr. $204 Principal for 1st half yr.

   B. $204 $204.00
      ×.02   × 4.08
      $4.08 Interest for 2nd half yr. $208.08 Principal for 1st half of 2nd yr.

   C. $208.08 $208.08
      ×.02   × 4.16
      $4.1616 Interest for 1st half of 2nd yr. $212.24 Principal for 2nd half of 2nd yr.

   D. $212.24 $212.24
      ×.02   × 4.24
      $4.2448 Interest for 2nd half of 2nd yr. $216.48 Principal at end of 2nd half of 2nd yr.

TEST 2

DIRECTIONS: Each question or incomplete statement is followed by several suggested answers or completions. Select the one that BEST answers the question or completes the statement. *PRINT THE LETTER OF THE CORRECT ANSWER IN
THE SPACE AT THE RIGHT.*

1.   With a *tax rate* of .0200, a tax bill of $1050 corresponds to an *assessed valuation*   1._____
of
     A. $21,000   B. $52,500   C. $21   D. $1029

2.   A sales agent, after deducting his commission of 6%, remits $2491 to his   2._____
principal. The SALE amounted to
     A. $2809   B. $2640   C. $2650   D. $2341.54

3.   The percent equivalent of .0295 is   3._____
     A. 2.95%   B. 29.5%   C. .295%   D. 295%

4.   An angle of 105 degrees is a _____ angle.   4._____
     A. straight   B. acute   C. obtuse   D. reflex

5.   A quart is approximately sixty cubic inches. A cu. ft. of water weighs approxi-   5._____
mately sixty pounds. Therefore, a quart of water weights *approximately*
     A. 2 lbs.   B. 3 lbs.   C. 4 lbs.   D. 5 lbs.

6.   If the *same* number is added to both the numerator and the denominator of a   6._____
proper fraction, the
     A. value of the fraction is decreased
     B. value of the fraction is increased
     C. value of the fraction is unchanged
     D. effect of the operation depends on the original fraction

7.   The *lease common multiple* of 3, 8, 9, 12 is   7._____
     A. 36   B. 72   C. 108   D. 144

8.   On a bill of $100, the *difference* between a discount of 30% and 20% and a   8._____
discount of 40% and 10% is
     A. nothing   B. $2   C. $20   D. 20%

9.   1/3 percent of a number is 24. The NUMBER is   9._____
     A. 8   B. 72   C. 800   D. 7200

10. The cost of importing five dozen china dinner sets, billed at $32 per set, and   10._____
paying a duty of 40% is
     A. $224   B. $2688   C. $768   D. $1344

_____

SOLUTIONS TO ARITHMETICAL REASONING

1. Answer: (B) $52,500
    0200x = $1050   2x = $105,000
    200x = $10,500,000   x = $52,500 (assessed valuation)

2. Answer: (C) $2650
    $2491 + .06x = x
    x = 2491 + .06x

                          Proof
    1.00x - .06x = 2491 $2650 $2491
                          × .06   + 159
                          $159.00 $2650

    .94x = 2491
    .94x = 249,100

        $2,650
    94)249,100

3. Answer: (A) 2.95% [.0295 = 2.95%)

4. Answer: (C) obtuse angle
    An obtuse angle is an angle greater than 90°.

5. Answer: (A) 2 lbs.
    A quart = 60 cu. in.
    60 lbs. = 1 cu. ft. (or 1728 cu. in.) (12×12×12)
            (Keep like units of measure together)
    60 lbs. = 1728 cu. in.
    1 lb.   = 1728/60 = approximately .29 cu. in.
    If 29 cu. in. weighs 1 lb., then 60 cu. in. weighs 2 lbs. (approximately). Therefore, a quart weighs 2 lbs. (approximately).

6. Answer: (B) the value of the fraction is increased

    (1) Start with the fraction 2/3

    (2) $\frac{2+2}{3+2} = \frac{4}{5}$ (Adding 2 to the numerator and the denominator)

    (3) $\frac{3}{2} = \frac{10}{15}$

    (4) $\frac{4}{5} = \frac{12}{15}$

7. Answer: (B) 72
    Common multiple can be evenly divided by all the numbers. Lease common multiple: the lowest of these numbers.

8.   Answer: (B) $2
     <u>Formula:</u>   Step 1. Express percentages as decimals
                   Step 2. Subtract each discount from *one*
                   Step 3. Multiply all the results
                   Step 4. Subtract the product from *one*

                   Step 1. .3, .2 and .4, .1
                   Step 2. .7, .8 and .6, .9
                   Step 3. .7 × .8 = .56 (represents percent remaining after the discounts
                        .6 × .9 = .54 are taken)
                   Step 4. 1.00   1.00
                            <u>-.56</u>   <u>-.54</u>
                             .44   .46

          Then, $100 × .02 = $2.00

9.   Answer: (D) 7200

     $\frac{1}{300}x = 24;$ x = 24×300;   x = 7200

10.   Answer: (B) $2688

          $32 $1920
          <u>×60</u>   <u>×.40</u>
          $1920 Cost of dinner sets before paying duty $768.00 Duty

          $1920
          <u>+ 768</u>
          $2688 Cost of dinner sets *after* paying duty

TEST 3

DIRECTIONS: Each question or incomplete statement is followed by several suggested answers or completions. Select the one that BEST answers the question or completes the statement. *PRINT THE LETTER OF THE CORRECT ANSWER IN THE SPACE AT THE RIGHT.*

1. A motorist travels 120 miles to his destination at the average speed of 60 miles per hour and returns to the starting point at the average speed of 40 miles per hour. His *average speed* for the ENTIRE trip is _____ miles per hour.
   A. 53   B. 50   C. 48   D. 45   1.____

2. A snapshot measures 2 1/2 inches by 1 7/8 inches. It is to be enlarged so that the longer dimension will be 4 inches. The length of the enlarged *shorter* dimension will be
   A. 2 1/2 inches   B. 3 3/8 inches   C. 3 inches   D. none of these   2.____

3. The approximate distance is, in feet, that an object falls in t seconds when dropped from a height is obtained by use of the formula $s = 16_t{}^2$. In 8 seconds, the object will fall
   A. 15,384 feet   B. 1,024 feet   C. 256 feet   D. none of these   3.____

4. The PRODUCT of 75^3 and 75^7 is
   A. $(75)^{10}$ B. $(75)^{21}$ C. $(5,625)^{10}$ D. $(150)^{10}$ 4.____

5. The scale of a map is: 3/4 of an inch = 10 miles. If the distance on the map between two towns is 6 inches, the *actual* distance is
   A. 45 miles   B. 60 miles   C. 80 miles   D. none of these   5.____

6. If $d = m \dfrac{50}{m}$, and m is a positive number which increases in value, d   6.____
   A. increases in value   B. decreases in value
   B. remains unchanged   D. fluctuates up and down in value

7. From a piece of tin in the shape of a square 6 inches on a side, the largest possible circle is cut out.
   Of the following, the ratio of the area of the circle to the area of the original square is *closest* in value to
   A. 4/5   B. 3/5   C. 2/3   D. 1/2   7.____

8. A pound of water is evaporated from 6 pounds of sea water containing 4% salt. The percentage of salt in the *remaining* solution is
   A. 3 1/3   B. 4   C. 4 4/5   D. none of these   8.____

9. If a cubic inch of a metal weighs 2 pounds, a cubic foot of the *same* metal weighs   9.____
   A. 8 pounds   B. 24 pounds   C. 288 pounds   D. none of these

10. Assume that, according to the Federal income tax law, if the taxable income in the case of a separate return is over $4,000, but not over $6,000, the tax is $840 + 26% of the excess over $4,000.
If a taxpayer files a separate tax return and his taxable income is $5,500, the tax is

    A. $690   B. $1,230   C. $1,370   D. none of these

SOLUTIONS TO ARITHMETICAL REASONING

1. Answer: (C) 48 miles per hour
    120 miles = 2 hours (60 mph)
    120 miles = 3 hours (40 mph)
    240 miles = 5 hours = average of 48 mph

2. Answer: (C) 3 inches
    Change 2 1/2 to 20/8   Change 1 7/8 to 15/8
    Ratio is 20 to 15 or 4 to 3.
    If the longer dimension is 4 inches, then the shorter is 3 inches.

3. Answer: (B) 1,024 feet
    s = 16 × 8^2 or 16 × 64 or 1024 feet

4. Answer: (A) $(75)^{10}$
    Because the 75 is constant, one needs only to add the exponents (7 and 3). There-fore, the product is 75^{10}.

5. Answer: (C) 80 miles
    6 ÷ 3/4 = 6 × 4/3 = 24/3 or 8
    8 × 10 miles = 80 miles

6. Answer: (A) increases in value
    By increasing the value of my (by substituting numbers for letters), it is obvious that d increases in value.

7. Answer: (A) 4/5
    Area of square = 36 square inches
    Area of circle = π^2
                   = π 9 (3 × 3)
                   = 3 1/7 × 9
                   = 28 2/7

$$\frac{28\ 2/7}{36} = \frac{198}{7} \times \frac{1}{36} = \frac{198}{252}$$

    .78 = 78%
    252)198.00
        176 4
         21 60
         20 16
          1 44

78% is closest to 4/5 (80%)

8. Answer: (C) 4 4/5
    .04 × 6 = .24 lbs. of salt in 6 lbs. of salt water
    When a pound of water is evaporated, the salt content remains the same.

    .24
    5).24
    .04   4/5 = 4 4/5%

9. Answer: (D) none of these
    1728 cubic inches   = 1 cubic foot
    1 cubic inch   = 2 pounds
    1728 cubic inches   = 3,456 pounds

10. Answer: (B) $1,230

    $5,500
    -4,000 $1500 × 25% = $390.00
    $1,500 (excess over 4000)   +840.00
                                                 $1230.00 (tax)

TEST 4

DIRECTIONS: Each question or incomplete statement is followed by several suggested answers or completions. Select the one that BEST answers the question or completes the statement. *PRINT THE LETTER OF THE CORRECT ANSWER IN THE SPACE AT THE RIGHT.*

1. If the number of square inches in the area of a circle is equal to the number of inches in its circumference, the DIAMETER of the circle is
   A. 4 inches   B. 3 inches   C. 1 inch   D. none of these

   1.____

2. The *least common multiple* of 20, 24, 32 is
   A. 900   B. 1,920   C. 15,360   D. none of these

   2.____

3. Six quarts of a 20% solution of alcohol in water are mixed with 4 quarts of a 60% solution of alcohol in water. The *alcoholic* strength of the mixture is
   A. 80%   B. 50%   C. 36%   D. none of these

   3.____

4. To find the radius of a circle whose circumference is 60 inches,
   A. multiply 60 by π
   B. divide 60 by 2π
   C. divide 30 by 2π
   D. divide 60 by π and extract the square root of the result

   4.____

5. A micromillimeter is defined as one millionth of a millimeter. A length of 17 micromillimeters may be represented by
   A. .00017 mm.   B. 0000017 mm.
   C. .000017 mm.   D. .00000017 mm.

   5.____

6. If $9x + 5 = 23$, the numerical value of $18x + 5$ is
   A. 46   B. 41   C. 32   D. 23 + 9x

   6.____

7. When the fractions 2/3, 5/7, 8/11 and 9/13 are arranged in ascending order of size, the result is
   A. 8/11, 5/7, 9/13, 2/3   B. 5/7, 8/11, 2/3, 9/13
   C. 2/3, 8/11, 5/7, 9/13   D. 2/3, 9/13, 5/7, 8/11

   7.____

8. If the outer diameter of a metal pipe is 2.84 inches and the inner diameter is 1.94 inches, the *thickness* of the metal is
   A. .45 of an inch   B. .90 of an inch   C. 1.94 inches   D. 2.39 inches

   8.____

9. An office manager employs 3 typists at $450 per week, 2 general clerks at $400 per week, and a messenger at $320 per week. The *average* weekly wage of these part-time employees is
   A. $372.50   B. $390.00   C. $411.70   D. none of these

   9.____

10. A rectangular bin 4 feet long, 3 feet wide, and 2 feet high is solidly packed with bricks whose dimensions are 8 inches, 4 inches, and 2 inches. The *number* of bricks in the bin is
    A. 54   B. 648   C. 1,298   D. none of these

    10.____

SOLUTIONS TO ARITHMETICAL REASONING

1. Answer: (A) 4 inches
   Assume there are 100 square inches in the area of a circle and 100 inches in its circumference.

   $$A = 1/2Cr$$
   $$100 = 1/2 \times Xr$$
   $$50r = 100$$
   $$r = 2$$
   $$d = 4$$

2. Answer: (D) none of these

   $$2)\overline{20 - 24 - 32}$$
   $$2)\overline{10 - 12 - 16}$$
   $$2)\overline{20 - 24 - 32}$$
   $$\quad\ \ 5 - 3 - 4$$

   $2 \times 2 \times 2 \times 5 \times 3 \times 4 = 480$

3. Answer: (C) 36%

6 quarts × 20%	=	120%
4 quarts × 60%	=	240%
10 quarts	=	360%
1 quart	=	36%

4. Answer: (B) divide 60 by 2

   $$C = 2r$$

   $$2\pi r = 60$$

   $$2r = \frac{60}{\pi}$$

   $$r = \frac{60}{\pi} \times \frac{1}{2}$$

   $$r = \frac{60}{2\pi}$$

5. Answer: (C) .000017 mm.
   1 micromillimeter = .000001 mm.
   17 micromillimeters = .000017 mm.

6. Answer: (B) 41
   $9x + 5 = 23$
   $9x = 23 - 5$ or $9x = 18$
   $x = 2$
   $18x + 5 = 36 + 5$ or 41

7. Answer: (D) 2/3, 9/13, 5/7, 8/11
   Find the least common denominator = 3003

   $$\frac{2}{3} = \frac{2002}{3003} \qquad \frac{9}{13} = \frac{2079}{3003} \qquad \frac{5}{7} = \frac{2145}{3003} \qquad \frac{8}{11} = \frac{2184}{3003}$$

   Correct order is 2/3, 9/13, 5/7, 8/11

8.   Answer: (A) .45 of an inch
       2.84 inches   =   outer diameter
       <u>1.94</u> inches   =   inner diameter
        .90 inches   =   thickness (both sides)
        .45 inches   =   thickness (one side)

9.   Answer: (C) $41.17
       3 × 45   = $135
       2 × 40   =   80

       $\dfrac{1}{6}$ × 32 = $\dfrac{32}{\$247}$

       $247 ÷ 6 = $41 1/6 or $41.17

10.   Answer: (B) 648

       There are 1728 cu. inches in 1 cu. ft. (12 × 12 × 12)
       4 × 3 × 2 = 24 cu.ft. × 1728 = 41472 cu. in. ÷ 64 (8 × 4 × 2) = 648 bricks

TEST 5

DIRECTIONS: Each question or incomplete statement is followed by several suggested answers or completions. Select the one that BEST answers the question or completes the statement. *PRINT THE LETTER OF THE CORRECT ANSWER IN THE SPACE AT THE RIGHT.*

1. If x is less than 10, and y is less than 5, it follows that   1._____
    A. x is greater than y   B. x = 2y
    C. x-y = 5   D. x+y is less than 15

2. A dealer sells an article at a loss of 50% of the cost. Based on the selling   2._____
    price, the *loss* is
    A. 25%   B. 50%
    C. 100%   D. none of these

3. If 8 men get together at a reunion and each man shakes hands once with   3._____
    each of the others, the *total number* of handshakes is
    A. 49   B. 56   C. 64   D. 28

4. The world record for cycling a stretch of 20 kilometers is 26 minutes. This   4._____
    corresponds to an average speed of, *approximately*,
    A. 29 miles per hour   B. 46 miles per hour
    C. 32 miles per hour   D. none of these

5. The sum, s, of n consecutive integers beginning with 1 can be found by use   5._____

    of the formula s = $\frac{n(n+1)}{2}$. The sum of the *first 100 consecutive integers* is

    A. 5,001   B. 5,050   C. 10,000   D. 10,100

6. Of the following, the value of $\dfrac{\sqrt[3]{64.32}}{\sqrt{.041}}$ is closest to   6._____

    A. 400   B. 200   C. 20   D. 16

7. If each edge of a cube is increased by 2 inches, the   7._____
    A. volume is increased by 8 cubic inches
    B. area of each face is increased by 4 square inches
    C. diagonal of each face is increased by 2 inches
    D. sum of the edges is increased by 24 inches

8. In a school in which 40% of the enrolled students are boys, 80% of the boys   8._____
    are present on a certain day. If 1,152 boys are present, the total school en-
    rollment is
    A. 1,440   B. 2,880
    C. 3,600   D. none of these

9. An agent received a commission of d% of the selling price of a house. If the
commission amounted to $600, the selling price, in dollars, was

    A. $\frac{60,000}{d}$ B. 600/d   C. 6d   D. 600d

9.____

10. A ship sails due north from a position 5 28' South Latitude to a position 6 43'
North Latitude. Given that one minute of latitude is equivalent to 1 nautical
mile, the ship has sailed a distance of _____ nautical miles

    A. 75   B. 371   C. 731   D. 1,211

10.____

SOLUTIONS TO ARITHMETICAL REASONING

1.   Answer: (D) x + y is less than 15
     If x is less than 10 and y is less than 5, then x + y *MUST* be less than 15. None of the others is possible.

2.   Answer: (C) 100%
     Based on selling price, the formula is written:
     Cost – Loss = Selling Price
     100% - 50% = 50%
     Loss = 100% of the Selling Price (loss equal to Selling Price)

3.   Answer: (D) 28
     A shakes hands with the other 7
     B shakes hands with the other 6 (has already shaken A's)
     and so on……. Thus 7, 6, 5, 4, 3, 2, 1 = 28 handshakes

4.   Answer: (A) 29 miles per hour
     1 kilometer = 5/8 of a mile
     20 kilometers = 20 × 5/8 = 12 1/2 miles
     12 1/2 miles : 26 minutes   =   x : 60 minutes
                         26x   =   750
                           x   =   28+ or 29 miles per hour

5.   Answer: (B) 5,050

$$s = \frac{n(n+1)}{2} \qquad s = \frac{100(100+1)}{2} \qquad s = \frac{10,100}{2} \qquad s = 5,050$$

6.   Answer: (C) 2

$$\sqrt[3]{64.32} = 4.01 \qquad\qquad \frac{4}{.2} = 4 \times \qquad \frac{10}{2} = 20$$

$$\sqrt[2]{.041} \quad - .202$$

7.   Answer: (D) the sum of the edges is increased by 24 inches. Since there are 12 edges to a cube and each edge is increased by 2 inches, the total increase is 24 inches.

8.   Answer: (C) 3,600

$$1152 \div \frac{8}{10} = 1440 = 1440 \text{ boys enrolled } (1152 \times 10/8)$$

$$1440 \div \frac{4}{10} = 1440 \times \frac{10}{4} \quad \text{(total school enrollment)}$$

9.   Answer: (A) $\dfrac{60,000}{d}$

$$600 \div d = 600 \times \frac{100}{d} = \frac{60,000}{d}$$

10. Answer: (C) 731 nautical miles

5° 28'	1° = 60'
6° 43'	11° = 660'
11° 71'	+ 71'
	731'

1' = 1 nautical mile
731' = 731 nautical miles

EXAMINATION SECTION

DIRECTIONS: Each question or incomplete statement is followed by several suggested answers or completions. Select the one that BEST answers the question or completes the statement. *PRINT THE LETTER OF THE CORRECT ANSWER IN THE SPACE AT THE RIGHT.*

1. 2/3 x 12 equals

   1._____

   A. 4   B. 6   C. 8
   D. 18   E. None of the above

2. 83.97
    1.78
   14.36
    9.03

   2._____

   The sum of the above column is

   A. 99.13   B. 99.24   C. 109.14
   D. 109.23   E. 109.24

3. The value of x in the equation 5x = 75 is

   3._____

   A. 13   B. 15   C. 70
   D. 80   E. none of the above

4. 65.13 ÷ .13 equals

   4._____

   A. .501   B. 5.01   C. 50.1
   D. 501   E. none of the above

5. The sum of 6 feet 8 inches and 3 feet 4 inches is

   5._____

   A. 2 ft. 2 in.   B. 9 ft.   C. 10 ft.
   D. 10 ft. 12 in.   E. none of the above

6. 3/4 - 1/2 + 1/8 equals

   6._____

   A. 3/10   B. 3/8   C. 5/8
   D. 1 3/8   E. none of the above

7. 4 5/16 - 2 3/8 equals

   7._____

   A. 1 15/16   B. 2 1/16   C. 2 1/4
   D. 2 15/16   E. none of the above

8. (-12) + (-3) equals

   8._____

   A. -9   B. +15   C. +9
   D. -15   E. none of the above

9. The ratio of the lengths of two lines is 5 to 3. The length of the shorter line is 30 inches. The length of the longer line is _____ inches.

   9._____

   A. 18   B. 48   C. 50
   D. 150   E. none of the above

10. .025 written as a common fraction is

   10._____

A.	25/10	B.	25/100	C.	25/1000
D.	25/10,000	E.	none of the above		

11. In the proportion 5/2 = 9/x the value of x is   11._____

A.	1.8	B.	3.6	C.	22.5
D.	36	E.	none of the above		

12. 33 1/3 percent of 3 equals   12._____

A.	1	B.	10	C.	100/3
D.	100	E.	none of the above		

13. $\sqrt{225}$ equals   13._____

A.	15	B.	20.5	C.	25
D.	112.5	E.	none of the above		

14. On the portion of the scale shown at the right, the reading to which the arrow points is _____ units.   14._____
   A. 6 3/16
   B. 6 3/5
   C. 6 3/4
   D. 7 5/8
   E. none of the above

15. If 4x/5 - 6 = 10, then x equals   15._____

A.	15 1/5	B.	5	C.	4
D.	3 1/5	E.	none of the above		

16. The difference between 8 hours 0 minutes 6 seconds and 6 hours 4 minutes 15 seconds is _____ hr. _____ min. _____ seconds.   16._____

A.	0; 54; 51	B.	1; 54; 51	C.	2; 4; 9
D.	2; 54; 45	E.	none of the above		

17. The scores made by nine pupils on a science test are: 2, 4, 6, 6, 8, 10, 12, 14, 19. The MEAN score is   17._____

A.	6	B.	8	C.	9
D.	81	E.	none of the above		

18. A certain cost formula is represented graphically in the figure at the right. From the graph, when n = 7, the value of C is about   18._____
   A. 140
   B. 120
   C. 110
   D. 102
   E. none of the above

106

19. A simplified form of the expression A = 1/2 bh + 1/2 ah is

    A.   A = 1/2 h(b+a)   B.   A = bh + ah   C.   A = abh

    D. $\dfrac{A}{\frac{1}{2}bh} = \dfrac{1}{2}ah$ E.   none of the above

19.____

20. The ratio of 6 inches to 3 feet is

    A.   6/1   B.   2/1   C.   1/2
    D.   1/18   E.   none of the above

20.____

21. The value of s in the equation 3s = 12 - s is

    A.   6   B.   4   C.   3 2/3
    D.   3   E.   none of the above

21.____

22. 16 2/3 percent of what number is 30?

    A.   5   B.   18   C.   160
    D.   180   E.   none of the above

22.____

23. The line graph shown at the right represents the temperature readings in Albany, New York, at two-hour intervals from 4 A.M. to 10 P.M. on a certain day in February. The APPROXIMATE change in temperature between 7 A.M. and 9 A.M. is _____ degrees.

    A.   3.5
    B.   3.0
    C.   2.5
    D.   2.0
    E.   none of the above

23.____

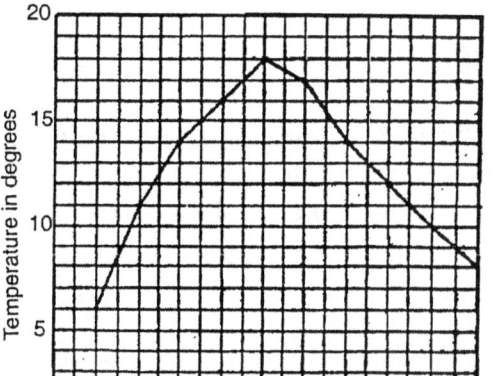

Questions 24-25.

DIRECTIONS: Questions 24 and 25 are to be answered on the basis of the following figure and information.

In the figure below, a square whose side is b is cut from a square whose side is a.

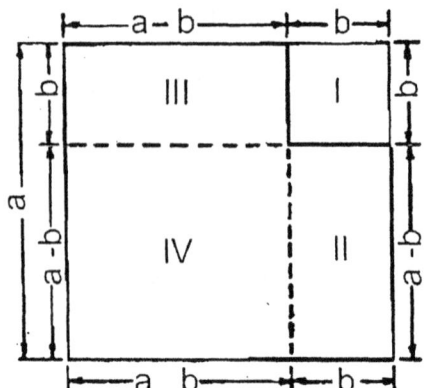

24. The sum of the perimeters of Section I and Section III can be represented by   24.____

    A. b^2 B. 4a - 2b   C. 2a + 3b
    D. a(a-b)   E. none of the above

25. The sum of the areas of Section II and Section IV can be represented by   25.____

    A. b^2 B. 4a - 2b   C. 2a + 3b
    D. a(a-b)   E. none of the above

26. The temperature reading (F) on the Fahrenheit scale equals 32 more than 9/5 of the   26.____
Centigrade reading (C).
This rule when translated into symbols is expressed by

    A. F = 9/5C + 32   B. F = 9/5(C + 32)   C. F = 9/5 + 32C
    D. F + 32 = 9/5C   E. none of the above

27. In the equation 6x - 114 = .3x, the value of x is   27.____

    A. 38   B. 20   C. 12 2/3
    D. 2   E. none of the above

28. What percent of 42 is 84?   28.____

    A. 4%   B. 2%   C. 50%
    D. 200%   E. none of the above

29. The CORRECT name of the solid figure at the right is   29.____
    A.   semicircle
    B.   circle
    C.   sphere
    D.   cone
    E.   cylinder

30. Which of these fractions has the LARGEST value?   30.____

    A. 1/2   B. 5/9   C. 7/12
    D. 2/3   E. 3/4

31. The formula for the area of a circle is A =   31.____

    A. πr^2 B. $2/3\,\pi r^2$ C. $2\pi r$
    D.   bh   E.   none of the above

32. The CORRECT name of the figure at the right is   32.____

    A.   pentagon
    B.   hexagon
    C.   rectangle
    D.   trapezoid
    E.   square

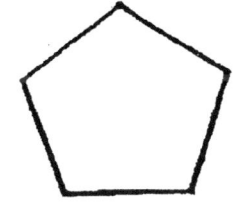

33. The figure at the right is a   33.____

    A.   rectangle
    B.   square
    C.   pentagon
    D.   trapezoid
    E.   parallelogram

34. If x = -18, y = 3, and z = -2, then x - y + z equals   34.____

    A. 3   B. -3   C. -23   D. -52   E. -56

35. The number 335,560 rounded off to the nearest thousand is   35.____

    A.   335,000   B.   335,500   C.   336,000
    D.   340,000   E.   none of the above

36. In the triangle ABC at the right, the sum of the angles is _____ degrees.   36.____

    A.   360
    B.   180
    C.   90
    D.   45
    E.   none of the above

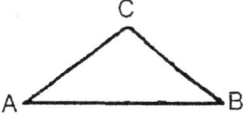

37. According to the map shown at the right, the
APPROXIMATE distance between the southern
point of New York City and Albany is _____.
miles.
A. 50
B. 75
C. 130
D. 180
E. 200

37.____

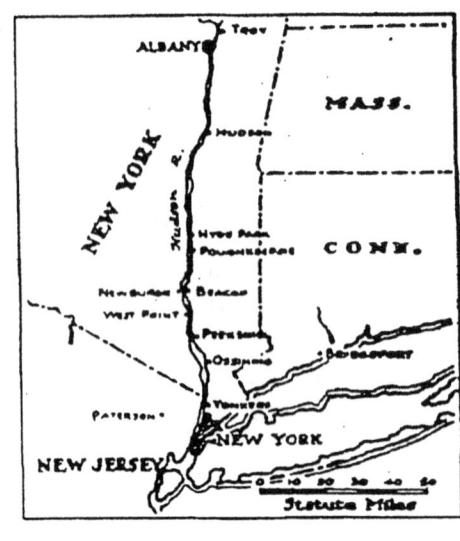

38. If 6 is added to a certain number n, the result is 1. An equation which expresses this relationship is

38.____

A. $n + 6 = 1$ B. $n - 1 = 6$ C. $6 - n = 1$
D. $n + 1 = 6$ E. none of the above

39. In the expression $2n^3$, the 3 is called a(n)

39.____

A. coefficient   B. factor   C. exponent
D. multiplicand   E. none of the above

40. The number of inches in n feet is represented by

40.____

A. 12n   B. 3n   C. n/3
D. n/12   E. none of the above

41. The simple interest on $600 for 3 months at 4 percent per year is represented by 600 x
.04 x

41.____

A. 1/4   B. 1/3   C. 3
D. 4   E. none of the above

42. The circle graph at the right indicates
how a family's annual budget of $3000
was planned.

42.____

Food   40 percent
Shelter   25 percent
Clothes   15 percent
Operating Expenses   10 percent
Insurance & Savings   10 percent
The part of the circle representing Shelter is _____ degrees.

A. 25   B. 45   C. 90   D. 250
E. none of the above

110

43. In the parallelogram ABCD at the right, each small square represents 4 square inches.
The area of the right triangle AED represents _____ square inches.

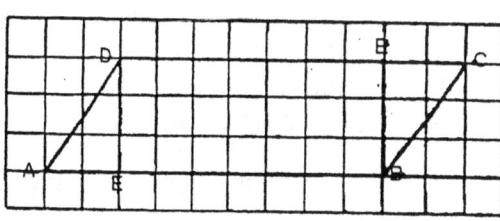

43.____

    A.   3   B.   12   C.   24   D.   48
    E.   none of the above

44. A surveyor measured angle x with a transit. (See figure at the right.) Angle x is called

44.____

    A.   the angle of depression of B from A
    B.   an obtuse angle
    C.   the supplement of angle
    D.   the angle of elevation of B from A
    E.   none of the above

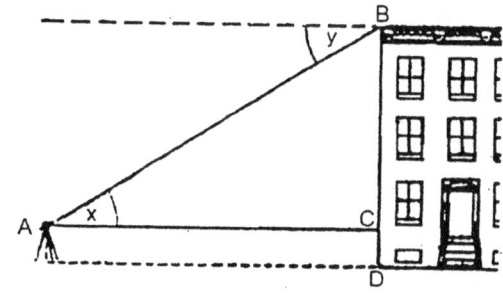

45. In the figure at the right, AOB is a straight line. An equation showing the relationship between u and v is

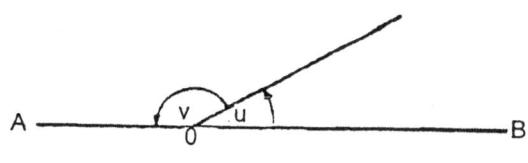

45.____

    A.   u = 1/2 v
    B.   u = 180 - v
    C.   u + v = 90
    D.   v = 3u
    E.   none of the above

46. If x = 4 when y = 6 and x varies directly as y, then when y = 15, x equals

46.____

    A.   20   B.   10   C.   1 3/5   D.   1 1/3
    E.   none of the above

47. A discount of 15 percent from a marked price produces a net price which is _____ of the marked price.

47.____

    A.   .15%   B.   .85%   C.   15%   D.   85%   E.   115%

48. When the formula A = P + Prt is solved for t, t equals

48.____

    A.   A - P - Pr   B. $\dfrac{A - Pr}{P}$ C. $\dfrac{A - P}{1 + r}$

    D. $\dfrac{A - P}{Pr}$ E.   none of the above

49. The Greek letter π

    A. was assigned the value 3.1416 by the International Court of Law
    B. was given an arbitrary value of 22/7 by a famous mathematician
    C. was discovered to be exactly 3.142
    D. when multiplied by the radius of a circle equals the area
    E. is used as a symbol for the ratio of the circumference of a circle to its diameter

50. If the base and altitude of a triangle are doubled, the area

    A. remains constant   B. is multiplied by 4
    C. is doubled   D. is divided by 4
    E. is none of the above

51. Each side of the equilateral triangle in the figure at the right is s inches long. The length of an altitude of the triangle is represented as

    A. s in.

    B. $s\sqrt{2}$ in.

    C. $s\sqrt{3}$ in.

    D. $\dfrac{s\sqrt{3}}{2}$ in.

    E. none of the above

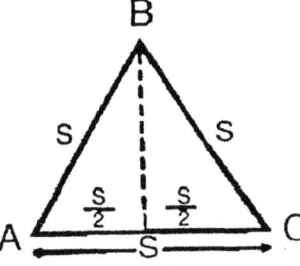

52. The length of a meter is about _____ inches.

    A. 1   B. 6   C. 12   D. 40   E. 100

53. A point which lies on the straight-line graph of the equation 2x - 3y = 12 is

    A. (3,-2)   B. (2,-3)   C. (-4,0)
    D. (0,6)   E. none of the above

54. If the two parallel lines AB and CD in the figure at the right are cut by a third line, EF, then the FALSE statement is

    A. $\angle r + \angle s = \angle s + \angle y$

    B. $\angle y + \angle w = \angle t + \angle s$

    C. $\angle u + \angle w = \angle s + \angle x$

    D. $\angle r + \angle x = \angle t + \angle w$

    E. $\angle s + \angle u = \angle r + \angle t$

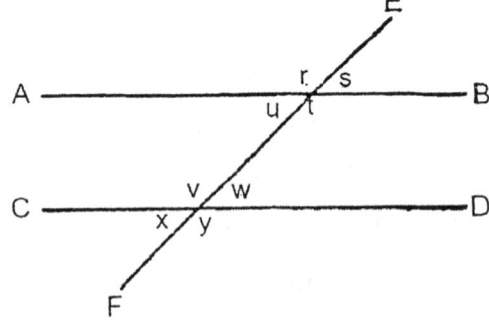

55. The product of n^4 and n^2 equals

    A. $2n^8$ B. $2n^6$ C. n^8
    D. n^2 E. none of the above   F.

55._____

56. The volume of the rectangular solid shown at the right is

    A. 12 cu. in.
    B. 44 sq. in.
    C. 48 cu. in.
    D. 88 sq. in.
    E. none of the above

56._____

57. Baseball bats listed at twenty-one dollars per dozen are sold to schools at a discount of 20 percent.
How much do they cost the schools per dozen?

    A. $4.20   B. $16.80   C. $20.80
    D. $25.20   E. None of the above

57._____

58. Last year a Chicago merchant's total business amounted to $30,000. For the goods sold, he paid $12,000, for rent he paid $2500, for clerk services $4742, and for other expenses $1058.
His average monthly net profit was

    A. $676.67   B. $891.67   C. $2500.00
    D. $9700.00   E. none of the above

58._____

59. If the marked price of an article is $100 and the first discount is 10 percent and the second discount 2 percent, the sale price is

    A. $78.20   B. $88.00   C. $88.20
    D. $88.80   E. none of the above

59._____

60. Mr. Smith agreed to pay an automobile agency a commission of 18 percent of the selling price of his car.
If the selling price was $1250, Mr. Smith would receive

    A. $225.00   B. $1025.00   C. $1227.50
    D. $1475.00   E. none of the above

60._____

61. Mr. Browne receives $30.45 per year on an investment of $870.
At this rate, if his total investment was $1500, his annual interest would be

    A. $52.50   B. $62.50   C. $625.00
    D. $655.45   E. none of the above

61._____

62. The Ephrata National Bank discounted a 60-day note for $3500 at 3 1/2 percent per year.   62.____
    The proceeds of the note were

    A. $3377.50   B. $3479.58   C. $3520.42
    D. $3622.50   E.   none of the above

63. The normal weight of an adult can be found by using the formula $w = 5.5(20+d)$, where w 63.____
    represents the weight in pounds and d the number of inches one's height exceeds 5 feet.
    By this formula, the normal weight of an adult who is 5'6" tall is _____ pounds.

    A.   134   B.   140.25   C.   140.8
    D.   143.0   E.   none of the above

64. In the figure at the right, triangles ACB and ADE are   64.____
    similar triangles. The length of side DE is _____ feet.
    A.   30
    B.   32
    C.   48
    D.   50
    E.   none of the above

65. A square piece of tin shown in the figure at the right   65.____
    is used to make an open box. One-inch squares are
    cut from each corner of the piece of tin and the sides
    then turned up, to form a box containing 49 cubic
    inches.
    The length of a side of the original square piece of tin
    required to make this box is _____ inches.

    A.   5
    B.   7
    C.   8
    D.   9
    E.   none of the above

KEY (CORRECT ANSWERS)

1.	C	16.	E	31.	A	46.	B	61.	A
2.	C	17.	C	32.	A	47.	D	62.	B
3.	B	18.	A	33.	E	48.	D	63.	D
4.	D	19.	A	34.	C	49.	E	64.	B
5.	C	20.	E	35.	C	50.	B	65.	D
6.	B	21.	D	36.	B	51.	D		
7.	A	22.	D	37.	C	52.	D		
8.	D	23.	C	38.	A	53.	A		
9.	C	24.	E	39.	C	54.	E		
10.	C	25.	D	40.	A	55.	E		
11.	B	26.	A	41.	A	56.	C		
12.	A	27.	B	42.	C	57.	B		
13.	A	28.	D	43.	B	58.	E		
14.	E	29.	E	44.	D	59.	C		
15.	E	30.	E	45.	B	60.	B		

SOLUTIONS TO PROBLEMS

1. $2/3 \times 12 = \dfrac{12}{1} = \dfrac{24}{3} = 8$ 1.____

2. Adding, we get 109.14   2.____

3. If $5x = 75$, $x = 75/5 = 15$ 3.____

4. $65.13 \div 13 = 501$ 4.____

5. 6 ft. 8 in. + 3 ft. 4 in. = 9 ft. 12 in. = 10 ft.   5.____

6. $3/4 - 1/2 + 1/8 = 6/8 - 4/8 + 1/8 = 3/8$ 6.____

7.____

7. $4\dfrac{15}{16} - 2\dfrac{3}{8} = 3\dfrac{21}{16} - 2\dfrac{6}{16} = 1\dfrac{15}{16}$

8. $(-12) + (-3) = -15$ 8.____

9. Let x = length of longer line. Then, $5:3 = x:30$. Solving, $x = 50$ 9.____

10. $.025 = 25/1000$ (Can also be reduced to $1/40$)   10.____

11. Cross-multiplying, $5x = 18$. Thus, $x = 18/5 = 3.6$ 11.____

12. $33\,1/3\%$ of $3 = (1/3)(3) = 1$ 12.____

13. $\sqrt{225} = 15$, since $15^2 = 225$ 13.____

14. The arrow points to $6\,3/8$ 14.____

15. $4x/5 - 6 = 10$. Adding 6, $4x/5 = 16$. Then, $x = 16 \div 4/5 = 20$ 15.____

16. 8 hrs. 0 min. 6 sec. - 6 hrs. 4 min. 15 sec. can be written as 7 hrs. 59 min. 66 sec. - 6 hrs. 4 min. 15 sec. to get 1 hr. 55 min. 51 sec.   16.____

17. Mean $= (2+4+6+6+8+10+12+14+19) \div 9 = 9$ 17.____

18. When $n = 0$, $c = 0$. When $n = 5$, $c = 100$. Thus, $c = 20n$. Finally, for $n = 7$, $c = (20)(7) = 140$ 18.____

19. $A = 1/2\,bh + 1/2\,ah = 1/2\,h(b+a)$ 19.____

20. 6 inches : 3 feet = 6 inches : 36 inches = $1/6$ 20.____

21. Add 5 to both sides to get $4s = 12$, so $s = 3$ 21.____

22. $16\,2/3\%$ of x is 30. Then, $1/6\,x = 30$, so $x = 180$ 22.____

23. At 7:00 AM the temperature was 12.5, while at 9:00 AM the temperature was 15. The change was 2.5 degrees.   23.____

24. Perimeter of Section I is 4b and the perimeter of Section III is 2b + 2a - 2b = 2a. The sum   24.____
    of the perimeters is 4b + 2a.

25. Area of Section II is b(a-b) = ab - b^2 and the area of Section IV is (a-b)^2 = a^2 - 2ab + b^2 .   25.____
    The sum of the areas is a^2 - ab = a(a-b).

26. Direct translation of words to symbols yields F = 9/5 C + 32   26.____

27. Subtract 6x to get -114 = -5.7x. Solving, x = 20   27.____

28. (84/42)(100)% = 200%   28.____

29. The figure is a cylinder.   29.____

30. Converting each choice to a decimal, we get .5, .$\overline{5}$, .58$\overline{3}$, .6, .75. The largest is .75 corre-   30.____
    sponding to 3/4.

31. For a circle, A = πr^2.   31.____

32. A five-sided enclosed figure with straight sides is called a pentagon.   32.____

33. A quadrilateral with opposite sides parallel is called a parallelogram. Rectangles and   33.____
    squares are parallelograms with 90° angles.

34. x - y + z = -18 - 3 - 2 = -23   34.____

35. Since the digit in the hundreds place is 5 or greater, the answer is 336,000.   35.____

36. The sum of the angles of any triangle is 180°.   36.____

37. The scale difference is about 2 inches, and since 50 miles corresponds to 3/4 inch, the   37.____
    actual distance is about (50) (2 ÷ 3/4) = 133 1/3 mi. Closest answer given is 130 mi.

38. 6 added to n means 6 + n. Thus, 6 + n = 1 or n + 6 = 1.   38.____

39. 3 is an exponent for 2n^3.   39.____

40. 12 inches in 1 foot means 12n inches in n feet.   40.____

41. 3 months = 1/4 year.   41.____

42. 25% of 360 degrees = 90 degrees   42.____

43. Area of $\triangle$ AED = (1/2)(2)(3) = 3 square units = 12 sq. inches   43.____

44. Angle x is the angle of elevation to B from A.   44.____

45. Since u + v = 180, we can also write u = 180 - v   45.____

46. 4/x = 6/15 Cross-multiplying, 6x = 60. Solving, x = 10   46.____

47. 100% - 15% = 85%   47.____

48. A = P + Prt becomes A - P = Prt. Dividing by Pr we get: t = (A-P)/Pr   48.____

49. π = ratio of circumference to diameter of a circle

    49.____

50. Let B = base, H = altitude. Original area of triangle = 1/2BH. If new base and altitude are 2B and 2H, new area = 1/2(2B)(2H) = 2BH, which is 4 times the value of 1/2BH.

    50.____

51. Let x = altitude. Then, $x^2 + (s/2)^2 = s^2$. This becomes $3/4s^2 = x^2$. Solving, $x = s\sqrt{3}/2$

    51.____

52. 1 meter $\approx$ 39.37 inches $\approx$ 40 inches

    52.____

53. Substituting (3,-2), 2(3) - 3(-2) = 12. The other points do not lie on 2x - 3y = 12.

    53.____

54. The false statement is $\angle s + \angle u = \angle r + \angle t$ (It is only true that $\angle s = \angle u$ and $\angle r = \angle t$).

    54.____

55. $n^4 \cdot n^2 = n^6$, since exponents are added in multiplication

    55.____

56. Volume = (6)(4)(2) = 48 cu.in.

    56.____

57. ($21)(.80) = $16.80

    57.____

58. $30,000 - $12,000 - $2500 - $4742 - $1058 = $9700. The monthly amount is $9700 ÷ 12 = $808.33

    58.____

59. ($100)(.90) = $90. Then, ($90)(.98) = $88.20

    59.____

60. 1250 - (1250)(.18) = $1025

    60.____

61. $30.45/$870 = 3.5% Then, 3.5% of $1500 = $52.50

    61.____

62. (.035)(60/360) = .0058$\overline{3}$= discount for 60 days.
    The value of the note =(1 -.0058$\overline{3}$)($3500) = $3479.58

    62.____

63. W = 5.5(20 + 6) = (5.5)(26) = 143

    63.____

64. x/80 = 40/100. Solving, x = 32. Note that AD:AC = DE:BC

    64.____

65. When folded, each new side is $\sqrt{49} = 7$ inches. Thus, the original length (unfolded) was 7+1+1=9 inches.

    65.____

BASIC INFORMATION ON POLLUTION AND POLLUTANTS

CONTENTS

BASIC INFORMATION ON POLLUTION AND POLLUTANTS

Following Is background information on noise, water , air and pesticide-herbicide pollution, and on the recycling process through which students and other members of the community can take individual action against pollution.

I. NOISE

A. Decibel levels

The following are averages:

Shout - 90	Motorcycle - 110
Normal conversation - 50-60	Riveting gun - 130
Whisper - 20	Thunderclap - 120
Jet - 117	

B. Health

It has been shown in animal studies, however, that rats born of mothers exposed to noise pollution during pregnancy had more difficulty in learning maze patterns than rats born of unstressed mother

Well-informed scientists reckon that if city noise continues to rise as it is presently rising, by one decibel a year, everyone will be stone deaf by the year 2000.

Rats, under prolonged noise exposure, have turned homosexual.

Dr. D. Glass (NYU) and Dr. J.Singer (SUNY) have shown that repeated random and unpredictable noises produce irritation and frustration, as well as dramatic declines in work efficiency even after the noise is stopped. Their studies disproved the popular assumption that man can learn to adjust to almost any noise.

C. Costs

Silence seems to cost between 5 and 10 percent more on most products.

II. PESTICIDES/HERBICIDES

A. General

Elimination of the use of persistent toxic pesticides should be t he goal.

B. Definition

Persistent, toxic pesticides include the following:

DDT	Chlordane
Aldrin	Lindane
Endrin	Benzene
Heptachlor	Hexachloride
Texaphene	Dieldrin

and there are those chlorinated hydrocarbons that do not break down completely in a few days or even a few years into less harmful materials. Of pesticides, all are not persistent. All, however, are questionable.

C. Wildlife

It has been discovered that many forms of wildlife - brown pelicans, peregrine falcons, and bald eagles, to name a few --
(1) have large quantities of DDT In their systems, and eggs, and
(2) are, in some areas, no longer capable of reproducing.

D. DDT

DDT Is an active product in over 35 products.

Evidence of severe oceanic contamination is the fact that some seabirds which never approach land except to nest are sometimes more contaminated with DDT than land birds.

E. Sea Creatures

Some organisms are unbelievably sensitive to the chlorinated hydrocarbons. For instance, nearly half the population of brine shrimp is killed within three weeks at a concentration of one part per trillion DDT, or 1/1000 of a drop in a tank-car lot. Temperature-control mechanisms are upset in young salmon at a few parts per billion, and death in a natural competitive environment could easily be the result.

III. WATER POLLUTION

A. Eutrophication

Eutrophication is a process whereby nutrients (nitrates and phosphates) are added to the water in bodies of water, causing multiplication of algae and small bacterial plants, which, due to their numbers, die in huge quantities, and exhaust the oxygen supply in decomposition. The water's oxygen is depleted to the extent that all other forms of life are choked to death.

Very recently the soap and detergent industry contended that because it is not the only cause of lake eutrophication, it should not be asked to find substitutes for phosphates in its detergents.

B. Phosphates

Phosphates are nutrients found in many detergents in the follow-ing concentrations:

Axion (Colgate Palmolive)	- 3%
Biz (Procter and Gamble)	- 40.4%
Bio-Ad (Colgate)	- 35.5%
Salvo (Procter and Gamble)	- 30.71%
Oxydol(Procter and Gamble)	- 30.7%

Tide (Procter and Gamble)	- 30.6%
Bold (Procter and Gamble)	- 30.25%
Ajax Laundry (Colgate)	- 25.2%
Punch (Colgate)	- 25.8%
Drive (Lever)	- 25.3%
Dreft (Procter and Gamble)	- 24.5%
Gain (Procter and Gamble)	- 23.1%
Duz (Procter and Gamble)	- 23.15%
Bonus (Procter and Gamble)	- 22.3%
Breeze (Lever)	- 22.2%
Cheer (Procter and Gamble)	- 22.05
Fab (Colgate)	- 21.5%
Cold Power (Colgate)	- 19.9%
Cold Water All (Lever)	- 8.8%
Wisk (Lever)	- 7.6%
Diaper Pure (Boyle)	- 5.0%
Trend (Purex)	- 1.4%

(A low-phosphate product, some say, does not get clothes clean. The answer is to add a"water softener" to the wash, and performanc is good.)

C. Fish

Over 15 million fish died last year from water pollution.

D. Fire

The Cuyahoga River, because of the general irresponsibility of polluters, was so contaminated with flammable oil and petroleum byproducts, that it caught on fire.

IV. AIR POLLUTION

A. General

According to the U.S. Public Health Service, any community with a population of 50,000 or more, has *a* real problem with air pollution.

The effects of air pollution are directly experienced by the wore than half of our population liing in our great widespread urban-suburban cornplexes .

B. Cancer

It has been generally concluded that air pollution is one of the factors contributing to the steady increase of lung cancer.

According to the U.S. Public Health Service, skin cancer that developed on a mouse after its skin was painted with pollutants from urban air, was probably caused by those pollutants.

C. Smoking

A person breathing the city's air inhales as much benzopyrene, a cancer-inducing hydrocarbon, as he would if he smoked two packs of cigarettes a day.

D. Trees

Early in this century, fumes from smelting operations in the Duektown-Copper Hill area of Southeastern Tennessee virtually de-nunded 17,000 acres (27 sq. miles) of forest land and severely damagec another 30,000 acres. Much of the area, bare and eroded still, has been likened by a recent observer to "the back side of the Moon."

During the summer of 1969, Christmas tree plantations along the Maryland-West Virginia border suffered heavy foliage damage. Plant scientists are convinced that air pollution was the cause and a nearby power-generating station was the source of the trouble.

E. Breathing

Each breath you take carries some 40,000 particles of dust if you are surrounded by "clean country air, some 70,000 if you live in the city. Then come the noxious gases. The nation's cars daily release: 250,000 tons of carbon monoxide, 16,500 to 33,000 tons of hydrocarbons, and 4,000 to 12,000 tons of nitrogen oxides.

F. Industry

The burning of coal for heat and power sends 48,000 tons of sulphur dioxide into the air very day.

G. Cars

The automobile is the primary villain in air pollution. It accounts for at least 60% of the total air pollution in the U.S., 85% of the pollution in some of our sprawling urban areas.

In the United States, the automobile produces 90$ of all carbon monoxide pollution.

V. RECYCLING

Natural processes are a system of cycles. All things are a part of this system. When man takes natural resources to produce things, he often interrupts a cycle. The idea behind recycling is to channel an item, once used, back into the system, thereby recycling it.

Our objective is to begin to treat garbage and trash with due respect. Reduce the amount of waste you produce by considering what will happen to each thing you purchase. Packaging will play an important role here. Things like cellophane, waxed paper, styro-foam, and plastics are not bio-degradable, or easily recyclable, and should be avoided. Try and recycle all things you do not need.

When, considering recycling, first re-use the item in its original form (use a box again). If this is not possible, utilize it for its material content (sell old paper to waste-paper company), An empty garvage can is a sign of ecological living.
Here are some ideas for you to use when recycling:

A. <u>Paper</u> - Read magazines and newspapers in the library. Avoid paper towels, napkins, diapers, cupss plates. Write on both sides. Use lunch boxes instead of paper sacks. Re-use one plastic bag to wrap sandwiches, etc., in. Use popcorn or something bio-degradable to cushion shipped or mailed items.

B. <u>Bottles</u> - Purchase all bottled drinks and liquids in reusable bottles. You are paying for the "convenience" of throw-away bottles - increased disposal costs and destruction of the environment, as well as higher purchase prices. Coke costs . 85?/ fluid ounce in 16-oz. deposit bottles., and 1.02?/fluid oz. in 16-oz. one way, and 1.36? an oz. in 12-oz. aluminum cans. Ask your grocer to continue to stock deposit bottles, and return your bottles to him, or write to the National Soft Drink Association, 1128 16th Street N.W., Washington, D.C. 20036, and tell them to continue deposit bottles. A typical deposit bottle is returned about 20 times

C. <u>Cloth</u> - Give usable clothing to one of the charity organizations operating a second-hand store. Buy clothes at a secondhand store. Sell old cloth to rag companies. They usually pay about 3?/lb. The clothing industry requires a great deal of agricultural land.

D. <u>Organic Material</u> - Keep a bucket in your kitchen for your food scraps. Bury them in your yard about 6" deep so they won't attract flies or dogs. They will decompose and fertilize the soil. Grow your own food. By doing so, you completely eliminate many pack-aging and additive/pesticide/chemical problems.

———

GLOSSARY OF ENVIRONMENTAL TERMS

TABLE OF CONTENTS

GLOSSARY OF ENVIRONMENTAL TERMS

A

ABATEMENT - The method of reducing the degree or intensity of pollution, also the use of such a method.

ABSORPTION - The penetration of a substance into or through another. For example, in air pollution control, absorption is the dissolving of a soluble gas, present in an emission, in a liquid which can be extracted.

ACCELERATOR - In radiology, a device for imparting high velocity to charged particles such as electrons or protons. These fast particles can penetrate matter and are known as radiation.

ACCLIMATION - The physiological and behavioral adjustments of an organism to changes in its immediate environment.

ACCLIMATIZATION - The acclimation or adaptation of a particular species over several generations to a marked change in the environment.

ACTIVATED CARBON - A highly adsorbent form of carbon, used to remove odors and toxic substances from gaseous emissions. In advanced waste treatment, activated carbon is used to remove dissolved organic matter from waste water.

ACTIVATED SLUDGE - Sludge that has been aerated and subjected to bacterial action, used to remove organic matter from sewage.

ACTIVATED SLUDGE PROCESS - The process of using biologically active sewage sludge to hasten breakdown of organic matter in raw sewage during secondary waste treatment.

ACUTE TOXICITY - Any poisonous effect produced within a short period of time, usually up to 24-96 hours, resulting in severe biological harm and often death.

ADAPTATION - A change in structure or habit of an organism that produces better adjustment to the environment.

ADSORPTION - The adhesion of a substance to the surface of a solid or liquid. Adsorption is often used to extract pollutants by causing them to be attached to such adsorbents as activated carbon or silica gel. Hydrophobic, or water-repulsing adsorbents, are used to extract oil from waterways in oil spills.

ADULTERANTS - Chemicals or substances that by law do not belong in a food, plant, animal or pesticide formulation. Adulterated products are subject to seizure by the Food and Drug Administration.

ADVANCED WASTE TREATMENT - Waste water treatment beyond the secondary or biological stage that includes removal of nutrients such as phosphorus and nitrogen and a high percentage of suspended solids. Advanced waste treatment, known as tertiary treatment, is the *polishing stage* of waste water treatment and produces a high quality effluent.

AERATION - The process of being supplied or impregnated with air. Aeration is used in waste water treatment to foster biological and chemical purification.

AEROBIC - This refers to life or processes that can occur only in the presence of oxygen.

AEROSOL - A suspension of liquid or solid particles in the air.

AFTERBURNER - An air pollution abatement device that removes undesirable organic gases through incineration.

AGRICULTURAL POLLUTION - The liquid and solid wastes from all types of farming, including runoff from pesticides, fertilizers, and feedlots; erosion and dust from plowing animal manure and carcasses and drop residues and debris. It has been estimated that agricultural pollution in the U.S. has amounted to more than 2 1/2 billion tons per year.

AIR CURTAIN - A method for mechanical containment of oil spills. Air is bubbled through a perforated pipe causing an upward water flow that retards the spreading of oil. Air curtains are also used as barriers to prevent fish from entering a polluted body of water.

AIR MASS - A widespread body of air with properties that were established while the air was situated over a particular region of the earth's surface and that undergoes specific modification while in transit away from that region.

AIR MONITORING - (See MONITORING.)

AIR POLLUTION - The presence of contaminants in the air in concentrations that prevent the normal dispersive ability of the air and that interfere directly or indirectly with man's health, safety, or comfort or with the full use and enjoyment of his property.

AIR POLLUTION EPISODE - The occurrence of abnormally high concentrations of air pollutants usually due to low winds and temperature inversion and accompanied by an increase in illness and death. (See INVERSION.)

AIR QUALITY CONTROL REGION - An area designated by the Federal government where two or more communities - either in the same or different states - share a common air pollution problem. AIR QUALITY CRITERIA - The levels of pollution and lengths of exposure at which adverse effects on health and welfare occur.

AIR QUALITY STANDARDS - The prescribed level of pollutants in the outside air that cannot be exceeded legally during a specified time in a specified geographical area.

ALGAL BLOOM - A proliferation of living algae on the surface of lakes, streams or ponds. Algal blooms are stimulated by phosphate enrichment.

ALPHA PARTICLE - A positively charged particle emitted by certain radioactive materials. It is the least penetrating of the three common types of radiation (alpha, beta and gamma) and usually not dangerous to plants, animals, or man.

AMBIENT AIR - Any unconfined portion of the atmosphere; the outside air.

ANADROMOUS - Type of fish that ascend rivers from the sea to spawn.

ANAEROBIC - Refers to life or processes that occur in the absence of oxygen.

ANTICOAGULANT - A chemical that intereferes with blood clotting, often used as a rodenticide.

ANTI-DEGRADATION CLAUSE - A provision in air quality and water quality laws that prohibits deterioration of air or water quality in areas where the pollution levels are presently below those allowed.

AQUIFER - An underground bed or stratum of earth, gravel, or porous stone that contains water.

AQUATIC PLANTS - Plants that grow in water, either floating on the surface, growing up from the bottom of the body of water, or growing under the surface of the water.

AREA SOURCE - In air pollution, any small individual fuel combustion source, including any transportation sources. This is a general definition; area source is legally and precisely defined in Federal regulations. (See POINT SOURCE.)

ASBESTOS - A mineral fiber with countless industrial uses; a hazardous air pollutant when inhaled.

A-SCALE SOUND LEVEL - The measurement of sound approximating the auditory sensitivity of the human ear. The A-Scale sound level is used to measure the relative noisiness or annoyance of common sounds.

ASSIMILATION - Conversion or incorporation of absorbed nutrients into protoplasm. Also refers to the ability of a body of water to purify itself of organic pollution.

ATMOSPHERE - The layer of air surrounding the earth.

ATOMIC PILE - A nuclear reactor.

ATTRACTANT - A chemical or agent that lures insects or other pests by olfactory stimulation.

ATTRITION - Wearing or grinding down by friction. One of the three basic contributing processes of air pollution; the others are vaporization and combustion.

AUDIOMETER - An instrument for measuring hearing sensitivity.
AUTOTROPHIC - Self-nourishing: denoting those organisms capable of constructing organic matter from inorganic substances.

B

BACKFILL - The material used to refill a ditch or other excavation, or the process of doing so.
BACKGROUND LEVEL - With respect to air pollution, amounts of pollutants present in the ambient air due to natural sources.
BACKGROUND RADIATION - Normal radiation present in the lower atmosphere from cosmic rays and from earth sources.
BACTERIA - Single-celled microorganisms that lack chlorophyll. Some bacteria are capable of causing human, animal, or plant diseases; others are essential in pollution control because they break down organic matter in the air and in the water.
BAFFLE - Any deflector device used to change the direction of flow or the velocity of water, sewage, or products of combustion such as fly ash or coarse particulate matter. Also used in deadening sound.
BAGHOUSE - An air pollution abatement device used to trap particu-lates by filtering gas streams through large fabric bags, usually made of glass fibers.
BALING - A means of reducing the volume of solid waste by compaction.
BALLISTIC SEPARATOR - A machine that separates inorganic from organic matter in a com-posting process.
BAND APPLICATION - With respect to pesticides, the application of the chemical over or next to each row of plants in a field.
BAR SCREEN - In waste water treatment, a screen that removes large floating and suspended solids.
BASAL APPLICATION - With respect to pesticides, the application of the pesticide formulation on stems or trunks of plants just above the soil line.
BASIN - (See RIVER BASIN.)
BENTHIC REGION - The bottom of a body of water. This region supports the benthos, a type of life that not only lives upon, but contributes to the character of the bottom.
BENTHOS - The plant and animal life whose habitat is the bottom of a sea, lake, or river.
BERYLLIUM - A metal that when airborne has adverse effects on human health, it has been declared a hazardous air pollutant. It is primarily discharged by operations such as machine shops, ceramic and propellant plants and foundries.
BETA PARTICLE - An elementary particle emitted by radioactive decay that may cause skin burns. It is easily stopped by a thin sheet of metal.
BIOASSAY - The employment of living organisms to determine the biological effect of some substance, factor, or condition.
BIOCHEMICAL OXYGEN DEMAND (BOD) - A measure of the amount of oxygen consumed in the biological processes that break down organic matter in water. Large amounts of organic waste use up large amounts of dissolved oxygen, thus the greater the degree of pollution, the greater the BOD.
BIODEGRADABLE - The process of decomposing quickly as a result of the action of microor-ganisms.
BIOLOGICAL CONTROL - A method of controlling pests by means of introduced or naturally occurring predatory organisms, sterilization, or the use of inhibiting hormones, etc. rather than by mechanical or chemical means.
BIOLOGICAL OXIDATION - The process by which bacterial and other microorganisms feed on complex organic materials and decompose them. Self-purification of waterways and activated

sludge and trickling filter waste water treatment processes depend on this principle. The process is also called biochemical oxidation.

BIOMONITORING - The use of living organisms to test the suitability of effluent for discharge into receiving waters and to test the quality of such waters downstream from a discharge.

BIOSPHERE - The portion of the earth and its atmosphere capable of supporting life.

BIOSTABILIZER - A machine used to convert solid waste into compost by grinding and aeration.

BIOTA - All the species of plants and animals occurring within a certain area.

BLOOM - A proliferation of living algae and/or other aquatic plants on the surface of lakes or ponds. Blooms are frequently stimulated by phosphate enrichment.

BOD - The amount of dissolved oxygen consumed in five days by biological processes breakdown of organic matter in an effluent. (See BIOCHEMICAL OXYGEN DEMAND.)

BOG - Wet, spongy land usually poorly drained, highly acid, and rich in plant residue.

BOOM - A floating device that is used to contain oil on a body of water.

BOTANICAL PESTICIDE - A plant-produced chemical used to control pests; for example, nicotine, strychnine, or orpyrethrun.

BRACKISH WATER - A mixture of fresh and salt water.

BREEDER - A nuclear reactor that produces more fuel than it consumes.

BROADCAST APPLICATION - With respect to pesticides, the application of a chemical over an entire field, lawn, or other area.

BURIAL GROUND (GRAVEYARD) - A place for burying unwanted radioactive materials to prevent radiation escape, the earth or water acting as a shield. Such materials must be placed in water-tight, noncorrodible containers so the radioactive material cannot leach out and invade underground water supplies.

C

CADMIUM - (See HEAVY METALS.)

CARBON DIOXIDE (CO_2) - A colorless, odorless, nonpoisonous gas that is a normal part of the ambient air. CO_2 is a product of fossil fuel combustion, and some researchers have theorized that excess CO_2 raises atmospheric temperatures.

CARBON MONOXIDE (CO) - A colorless, odorless, highly toxic gas that is a normal byproduct of incomplete fossil fuel combustion. CO, one of the major air pollutants, can be harmful in small amounts if breathed over a certain period of time.

CARCINOGENIC - Cancer producing.

CATALYTIC CONVERTER - An air pollution abatement device that removes organic contaminants by oxidizing them into carbon dioxide and water through chemical reaction. Can be used to reduce nitrogen oxide emissions from motor vehicles.

CAUSTIC SODA - Sodium hydroxide (NaOH), a strongly alkaline, caustic substance used as the cleaning agent in some detergents. CELLS - With respect to solid waste disposal, earthen compartments in which solid wastes are dumped, compacted, and covered over daily with layers of earth.

CENTRIFUGAL COLLECTOR - Any of several mechanical systems using centrifugal force to remove aerosols from a gas stream. CFS - Cubic feet per second, a measure of the amount of water passing a given point.

CHANNELIZATION - The straightening and deepening of streams to permit water to move faster, to reduce flooding, or to drain marshy acreage for farming. However, channelization reduces the organic waste assimilation capacity of the stream and may disturb fish breeding and destroy the stream's natural beauty.

CHEMICAL OXYGEN DEMAND (COD) - A measure of the amount of oxygen required to oxidize organic and oxidizable inorganic compounds in water. The COD test, like the BOD test, is used to determine the degree of pollution in an effluent.

CHEMOSTERILANT - A pesticide chemical that controls pests by destroying their ability to reproduce.

CHILLING EFFECT - The lowering of the earth's temperature due to the increase of atmospheric particulates that inhibit penetration of the sun's energy.

CHLORINATED HYDROCARBONS - A class of generally long-lasting, broad-spectrum insecticides of which the best known is DDT, first used for insect control during World War II. Other similar compounds include aldrin, dieldrin, heptachlor, chlordane, lindane, endrin, mirex, benzene hexachloride (BHC), and toxaphene. The qualities of persistence and effectivenss against a wide variety of insect pests were long regarded as highly desirable in agriculture, public health and home uses. But later research has revealed that these same qualities may represent a potential hazard through accumulation in the food chain and persistence in the environment.

CHLORINATION - The application of chlorine to drinking water, sewage or industrial waste for disinfection or oxidation of undesirable compounds.

CHLORINATOR - A device for adding a chlorine-containing gas or liquid to drinking or waste water.

CHLORINE-CONTACT CHAMBER - In a waste treatment plant, a chamber in which effluent is disinfected by chlorine before it is discharged to the receiving waters.

CHLOROSIS - Yellowing or whitening of normally green plant parts. It can be caused by disease organisms, lack of oxygen or nutrients in the soil or by various air pollutants.

CHROMIUM - (See HEAVY METALS.)

CHRONIC - Marked by long duration or frequent recurrence, as a disease.

CLARIFICATION - In waste water treatment, the removal of turbidity and suspended solids by settling, often aided by centrifugal action and chemically induced coagulation.

CLARIFIER - In waste water treatment, a settling tank which mechanically removes settleable solids from wastes.

COAGULATION - The clumping of particles in order to settle out impurities; often induced by chemicals such as lime or alum.

COASTAL ZONE - Coastal waters and adjacent lands that exert a measurable influence on the uses of the sea and its ecology.

COD - (See CHEMICAL OXYGEN DEMAND)

COEFFICIENT OF HAZE (COH) - A measurement of visibility interference in the atmosphere.

COFFIN - A thick-walled container (usually lead) used for transporting radioactive materials.

COH - (See COEFFICIENT OF HAZE)

COLIFORM INDEX - An index of the purity of water based on a count of its coliform bacteria.

COLIFORM ORGANISM - Any of a number of organisms common to the intestinal tract of man and animals whose presence in waste water is an indicator of pollution and of potentially dangerous bacterial contamination.

COMBINED SEWERS - A sewerage system that carries both sanitary sewage and storm water runoff. During dry weather, combined sewers carry all waste water to the treatment plant. During a storm, only part of the flow is intercepted because of plant overloading; the remainder goes untreated to the receiving stream.

COMBUSTION - Burning. Technically, a rapid oxidation accompanied by the release of energy in the form of heat and light. It is one of the three basic contributing factors causing air pollution; the others are attrition and vaporization.

COMMINUTION - Mechanical shredding or pulverizing of waste, a process that converts it into a homogeneous and more manageable material. Used in solid waste management and in the primary stage of waste water treatment.

COMMINUTOR - A device that grinds solids to make them easier to treat.

COMPACTION - Reducing the bulk of solid waste by rolling and tamping.

COMPOST - Relatively stable decomposed organic material.

COMPOSTING - A controlled process of degrading organic matter by microorganisms. (1) mechanical - a method in which the compost is continuously and mechanically mixed and aerated. (a) ventilated cell - compost is mixed and aerated by being dropped through a vertical series of ventilated cells. (3) windrow - an open-air method in which compostable material is placed in windrows, piles, or ventilated bins or pits and occasionally turned or mixed. The process may be anaerobic or aerobic.

CONTACT PESTICIDE - A chemical that kills pests on contact with the body, rather than by ingestion (stomach poison).

CONTRAILS - Long, narrow clouds caused by the disturbance of the atmosphere during passage of high-flying jets. Proliferation of contrails may cause changes in the weather.

COOLANT - A substance, usually liquid or gas, used for cooling any part of a reactor in which heat is generated, including the core, the reflector, shield, and other elements that may be heated by absorption of radiation.

COOLING TOWER - A device to remove excess heat from water used in industrial operations, notably in electric power generation.

CORE - The heart of a nuclear reactor where energy is released.

COVER MATERIAL - Soil that is used to cover compacted solid waste in a sanitary landfill.

CULTURAL EUTROPHICATION - Acceleration by man of the natural aging process of bodies of water.

CURIE - A measure of radiation.

CUTIE-PIE - A portable instrument equipped with a direct reading meter used to determine the level of radiation in an area.

CYCLONE COLLECTOR - A device used to collect large-size particulates from polluted air by centrifugal force.

D

DDT - The first of the modern chlorinated hydrocarbon insecticides whose chemical name is 1,1,1-tricholoro-2,2-bis (p-chloriphenyl)- ethane. It has a half-life of 15 years, and its residues can become concentrated in the fatty tissues of certain organisms, especially fish. Because of its persistence in the environment and its ability to accumulate and magnify in the food chain, EPA has banned the registration and interstate sale of DDT for nearly all uses in the United States effective December 31, 1972.

DECIBEL (dB) - A unit of sound measurement.

DECOMPOSITION - Reduction of the net energy level and change in chemical composition of organic matter because of the actions of aerobic or anaerobic microorganisms.

DERMAL TOXICITY - The ability of a pesticide chemical to poison an animal or human by skin absorption.

DESALINIZATION - Salt removal from sea or brackish water.

DESICCANT - A chemical that may be used to remove moisture from plants or insects causing them to wither and die.

DETERGENT - Synthetic washing agent that, like soap, lowers the surface tension of water, emulsifies oils and holds dirt in suspension. Environmentalists have criticized detergents because most contain large amounts of phosphorus-containing compounds that contribute to the eutrophication of waterways.

DIATOMACEOUS EARTH (DIATOMITE) - A fine siliceous material resembling chalk used in waste water treatment plants to filter sewage effluent to remove solids. May also be used as inactive ingredients in pesticide formulations applied as dust or powder.

DIFFUSED AIR - A type of sewage aeration. Air is pumped into the sewage through a perforated pipe.

DIGESTER - In a waste water treatment plant, a closed tank that decreases the volume of solids and stabilizes raw sludge by bacterial action.

DIGESTION - The biochemical decomposition of organic matter. Digestion of sewage sludge takes place in tanks where the sludge decomposes, resulting in partial gasification, liquefaction, and mineralization of pollutants.

DILUTION RATIO - The ratio of the volume of water of a stream to the volume of incoming waste. The capacity of a stream to assimilate waste is partially dependent upon the dilution ratio.

DISINFECTION - Effective killing by chemical or physical processes of all organisms capable of causing infectious diseases. Chlorination is the disinfection method commonly employed in sewage treatment processes.

DISPERSANT - A chemical agent used to break up concentrations of organic material. In cleaning oil spills, dispersants are used to disperse oil from the water surface.

DISSOLVED OXYGEN (DO) - The oxygen dissolved in water or sewage. Adequately dissolved oxygen is necessary for the life of fish and other aquatic organisms and for the prevention of offensive odors. Low dissolved oxygen concentrations generally are due to discharge of excessive organic solids having high BOD, the result of inadequate waste treatment.

DISSOLVED SOLIDS - The total amount of dissolved material, organic and inorganic, contained in water or wastes. Excessive dissolved solids make water unpalatable for drinking and unsuitable for industrial uses.

DISTILLATION - The removal of impurities from liquids by boiling. The steam, condensed back into liquid, is almost pure water; the pollutants remain in the concentrated residue.

DOSE - In radiology, the quantity of energy or radiation absorbed.

DOSIMETER (DOSEMETER) - An instrument used to measure the amount of radiation a person has received.

DREDGING - A method for deepening streams, swamps, or coastal waters by scraping and removing solids from the bottom. The resulting mud is usually deposited in marshes in a process called filling. Dredging and filling can disturb natural ecological cycles. For example, dredging can destroy oyster beds and other aquatic life; filling can destroy the feeding and breeding grounds for many fish species.

DRY LIMESTONE PROCESS - A method of controlling air pollution caused by sulfur oxides. The polluted gases are exposed to limestone which combines with oxides of sulfur to form manageable residues.

DUMP - A land site where solid waste is disposed of in a manner that does not protect the environment.

DUST - Fine-grain particulate matter that is capable of being suspended in air.

DUSTFALL JAR - An open-mouthed container used to collect large particles that fall out of the air. The particles are measured and analyzed.

DYSTROPHIC LAKES - Lakes between eutrophic and swamp stages of aging. Such lakes are shallow and have high humus content, high organic matter content, low nutrient availability, and high BOD.

E

ECOLOGICAL IMPACT - The total effect of an environmental change, either natural or man-made, on the ecology of the area.

ECOLOGY - The interrelationships of living things to one another and to their environment or the study of such interrelationships. ECONOMIC POISONS - Those chemicals used to control insects, rodents, plant diseases, weeds, and other pests, and also to defoliate economic crops such as cotton. ECOSPHERE - (See BIOSPHERE)

ECOSYSTEM - The interacting system of a biological community and its non-living environment.

EFFLUENT - A discharge of pollutants into the environment, partially or completely treated or in its natural state. Generally used in regard to discharges into waters.

ELECTRODIALYSIS - A process that uses electrical current and an arrangement of permeable membranes to separate soluble minerals from water. Often used to desalinize salt or brackish water.

ELECTROSTATIC PRECIPITATOR - An air pollution control device that removes particulate matter by imparting an electrical charge to particles in a gas stream for mechanical collection on an electrode.

EMERGENCY EPISODE - (See AIR POLLUTION EPISODE)

EMISSION - (See EFFLUENT) (Generally used in regard to discharges into air.)

EMISSION FACTOR - The average amount of a pollutant emitted from each type of polluting source in relation to a specific amount of material processed. For example, an emission factor for a blast furnace (used to make iron) would be a number of pounds of particulates per ton of raw materials.

EMISSION INVENTORY - A list of air pollutants emitted into a community's atmosphere, in amounts (usually tons) per day, by type of source. The emission inventory is basic to the establishment of emission standards.

EMISSION STANDARD - The maximum amount of a pollutant legally permitted to be discharged from a single source, either mobile or stationary.

ENRICHMENT - The addition of nitrogen, phosphorus, and carbon compounds or other nutrients into a lake or other waterway that greatly increases the growth potential for algae and other aquatic plants. Most frequently, enrichment results from the inflow of sewage effluent or from agricultural runoff.

ENVIRONMENT - The sum of all external conditions and influences affecting the life, development, and, ultimately, the survival of an organism.

ENVIRONMENTAL IMPACT STATEMENT - A document prepared by a Federal agency on the environmental impact of its proposals for legislation and other major actions significantly affecting the quality of the human environment. Environmental impact statements are used as tools for decision making and are required by the National Environmental Policy Act.

EPIDEMIOLOGY - The study of diseases as they affect populations.

EROSION - The wearing away of the land surface by wind or water. Erosion occurs naturally from weather or runoff but is often intensified by man's land-clearing practices.

ESTUARIES - Areas where the fresh water meets salt water. For example, bays, mouths of rivers, salt marshes, and lagoons. Estuaries are delicate ecosystems; they serve as nurseries, spawning and feeding grounds for a large group of marine life and provide shelter and food for birds and wildlife.

EUTROPHICATION - The normally slow aging process by which a lake evolves into a bog or marsh and ultimately assumes a completely terrestrial state and disappears. During eutrophication, the lake becomes so rich in nutritive compounds, especially nitrogen and phosphorus, that algae and other microscopic plant life becomes superabundant, thereby *choking* the lake and causing it eventually to dry up. Eutrophication may be accelerated by many human activities.

EUTROPHIC LAKES - Shallow lakes, weed-choked at the edges and very rich in nutrients. The water is characterized by large amounts of algae, low water transparency, low dissolved oxygen and high BOD.

EVAPORATION PONDS - Shallow, artificial ponds where sewage sludge is pumped, permitted to dry and either removed or buried by more sludge.

F

FABRIC FILTERS - A device for removing dust and particulate matter from industrial emissions much like a home vacuum cleaner bag. The most common use of fabric filters is the baghouse.

FECAL COLIFORM BACTERIA - A group of organisms common to the intestinal tracts of man and of animals. The presence of fecal coliform bacteria in water is an indicator of pollution and of potentially dangerous bacterial contamination.

FEEDLOT - A relatively small, confined land area for raising cattle. Although an economical method of fattening beef, feedlots concentrate a large amount of animal wastes in a small area. This excrement cannot be handled by the soil as it could be if the cattle were scattered on open range. In addition, runoff from feedlots contributes excessive quantities of nitrogen, phosphorus, and potassium to nearby waterways, thus contributing to eutrophication.

FEN - A low-lying land area partly covered by water.

FILLING - The process of depositing dirt and mud in marshy areas to create more land for real estate development. Filling can disturb natural ecological cycles. (See DREDGING)

FILM BADGE - A piece of masked photographic film worn like a badge by nuclear workers to monitor an exposure to radiation. Nuclear radiation darkens the film.

FILTRATION - In waste water treatment, the mechanical process that removes particulate matter by separating water from solid material usually by passing it through sand.

FLOC - A clump of solids formed in sewage by biological or chemical action.

FLOCCULATION - In waste water treatment, the process of separating suspended solids by chemical creation of clumps or floes.

FLOWMETER - In waste water treatment, a meter that indicates the rate at which waste water flows through the plant.

FLUE GAS - A mixture of gases resulting from combustion and emerging from a chimney. Flue gas includes nitrogen oxides, carbon oxides, water vapor, and often sulfur oxides or particulates.

FLUORIDES - Gaseous, solid or dissolved compounds containing fluorine, emitted into the air or water from a number of industrial processes. Fluorides in the air are a cause of vegetation damage and, indirectly, of livestock damage.

FLUME - A channel, either natural or manmade, which carries water.

FLY ASH - All solids, including ash, charred paper, cinders, dust, soot or other partially incinerated matter, that are carried in a gas stream.

FOG - Liquid particles formed by condensation of vaporized liquids.

FOGGING - The application of a pesticide by rapidly heating the liquid chemical, thus forming very fine droplets with the appearance of smoke. Fogging is often used to destroy mosquitoes and blackflies.

FOOD WASTE - Animal and vegetable waste resulting from the handling, storage, sale, preparation, cooking and serving of foods; commonly called garbage.

FOSSIL FUELS - Coal, oil, and natural gas; so-called because they are derived from the remains of ancient plant and animal life.

FUME - Tiny solid particles commonly formed by the condensation of vapors of solid matter.

FUMIGANT - A pesticide that is burned or evaporated to form a gas or vapor that destroys pests. Fumigants are often used in buildings or greenhouses.

FUNGI - Small, often microscopic plants without chlorophyll. Some fungi infect and cause disease in plants or animals; other fungi are useful in stabilizing sewage or in breaking down wastes for compost.

FUNGICIDE - A pesticide chemical that kills fungi or prevents them from causing diseases, usually on plants of economic importance. (See PESTICIDE)

G

GAME FISH - Those species of fish sought by sports fishermen; for example, salmon, trout, black bass, striped bass, etc. Game fish are usually more sensitive to environmental changes and water quality degradation than *rough* fish.

GAMMA RAY - Waves of radiant nuclear energy. Gamma rays are the most penetrating of the three types of radiation and are best stopped by dense materials such as lead.

GARBAGE - (See FOOD WASTE)

GARBAGE GRINDING - A method of grinding food waste by a household disposal, for example, and washing it into the sewer system. Ground garbage then must be disposed of as sewage sludge.

GEIGER COUNTER - An electrical device that detects the presence of radioactivity.

GENERATOR - A device that converts mechanical energy into electrical energy.

GERMICIDE - A chemical or agent that kills microorganisms such as bacteria and prevents them from causing disease. Such compounds must be registered as pesticides with EPA.

GRAIN - A unit of weight equivalent to 65 milligrams or 2/1,000 of an ounce.

GRAIN LOADING - The rate of emission of particulate matter from a polluting source. Measurement is made in grains of particulate matter per cubic foot of gas emitted.

GREEN BELTS - Certain areas restricted from being used for buildings and houses; they often serve as separating buffers between pollution sources and concentrations of population.

GREENHOUSE EFFECT - The heating effect of the atmosphere upon the earth. Light waves from the sun pass through the air and are absorbed by the earth. The earth then reradiates this energy as heat waves that are absorbed by the air, specifically by carbon dioxide. The air thus behaves like glass in a greenhouse, allowing the passage of light but not of heat. Thus, many scientists theorize that an increase in the atmospheric concentration of CO_2 can eventually cause an increase in the earth's surface temperature.

GROUND COVER - Grasses or other plants grown to keep soil from being blown or washed away.

GROUNDWATER - The supply of freshwater under the earth's surface in an aquifer or soil that forms the natural reservoir for man's use.

GROUNDWATER RUNOFF - Groundwater that is discharged into a stream channel as spring or seepage water.

H

HABITAT - The sum total of environmental conditions of a specific place that is occupied by an organism, a population or a community.

HALF-LIFE - The time it takes certain materials, such as persistent pesticides or radioactive isotopes, to lose half their strength. For example, the half-life of DDT is 15 years; the half-life of radium is 1,580 years.

HAMMERMILL - A broad category of high speed equipment that uses pivoted or fixed hammers or cutters to crush, grind, chip, or shred solid wastes.

HARD WATER - Water containing dissolved minerals such as calcium, iron, and magnesium. The most notable characteristic of hard water is its inability to lather soap. Some pesticide chemicals will curdle or settle out when added to hard water.

HAZARDOUS AIR POLLUTANT - According to law, a pollutant to which no ambient air quality standard is applicable and that may cause or contribute to an increase in mortality or in serious illness. For example, asbestos, beryllium, and mercury have been declared hazardous air pollutants.

HEAT ISLAND EFFECT - An air circulation problem peculiar to cities. Tall buildings, heat from pavements, and concentrations of pollutants create a haze dome that prevents rising hot air from being cooled at its normal rate. A self-contained circulation system is put in motion that can be broken by relatively strong winds. If such winds are absent, the heat island can trap high concentrations of pollutants and present a serious health problem.

HEATING SYSTEM - The coldest months of the year when pollution emissions are higher in some areas because of increased fossil-fuel consumption.

HEAVY METALS - Metallic elements with high molecular weights, generally toxic in low concentrations to plant and animal life. Such metals are often residual in the environment and exhibit biological accumulation. Examples include mercury, chromium, calcium, arsenic, and lead.

HERBICIDE - A pesticide chemical used to destroy or control the growth of weeds, bush, and other undesirable plants. (See PESTICIDE)

HERBIVORE - An organism that feeds on vegetation.

HETEROTROPHIC ORGANISM - Organisms dependent on organic matter for food.

HIGH DENSITY POLYETHYLENE - A material often used in the manufacture of plastic bottles that produces toxic fumes if incinerated.

HI-VOLUME SAMPLER - A device used in the measurement and analysis of suspended particulate pollution. Also called a Hi-Vol.

HOT - A colloquial term meaning highly radioactive.

HUMUS - Decomposed organic material.

HYDROCARBONS - A vast family of compounds containing carbon and hydrogen in various combinations, found especially in fossil fuels. Some hydrocarbons are major air pollutants, some may be carcinogenic and others contribute to photochemical smog.

HYDROGEN SULFIDE (H_2S) - A malodorous gas made up of hydrogen and sulfur with the characteristic odor of rotten eggs. It is emitted in the natural decomposition of organic matter and is also the natural accompaniment of advanced stages of eutrophication. H_2S is also a byproduct of refinery activity and the combustion of oil during power plant operations. In heavy concentrations, it can cause illness.

HYDROLOGY - The science dealing with the properties, distribution, and circulation of water and snow.

I

IMPEDANCE - The rate at which a substance can absorb and transmit sound.

IMPLEMENTATION PLAN - A document of the steps to be taken to ensure attainment of environmental quality standards within a specified time period. Implementation plans are required by various laws.

IMPOUNDMENT - A body of water, such as a pond, confined by a dam, dike, floodgate, or other barrier.

INCINERATION - The controlled process by which solid, liquid, or gaseous combustible wastes are burned and changed into gases; the residue produced contains little or no combustible material.

INCINERATOR - An engineered apparatus used to burn waste substances and in which all the combustion factors - temperature, retention time, turbulence, and combusion air - can be controlled.

INERT GAS - A gas that does not react with other substances under ordinary conditions.

INERTIAL SEPARATOR - An air pollution control device that uses the principle of inertia to remove particulate matter from a stream of air or gas.

INFILTRATION - The flow of a fluid into a substance through pores or small openings. Commonly used in hydrology to denote the flow of water into soil material.

INOCULUM - Material such as bacteria placed in compost or other medium to initiate biological action.

INTEGRATED PEST CONTROL - A system of managing pests by using biological, cultural, and chemical means.

INTERCEPTOR SEWERS - Sewers used to collect the flows from main and trunk sewers and carry them to a central point for treatment and discharge. In a combined sewer system, where street runoff from rains is allowed to enter the system along with sewage, interceptor sewers allow some of the sewage to flow untreated directly into the receiving stream, to prevent the plant from being overloaded.

INTERSTATE CARRIER WATER SUPPLY - A water supply whose water may be used for drinking or cooking purposes aboard common carriers (planes, trains, buses, and ships) operating interstate. Interstate carrier water supplies are regulated by the Federal government.

INTERSTATE WATERS - According to law, waters defined as (1) rivers, lakes and other waters that flow across or form a part of state or international boundaries; (2) waters of the Great Lakes; (3) coastal waters - whose scope has been defined to include ocean waters seaward to the territorial limits and waters along the coastline (including inland streams) influenced by the tide.

INVERSION - An atmospheric condition where a layer of cool air is trapped by a layer of warm air so that it cannot rise. Inversions spread polluted air horizontally rather than vertically so that contaminating substances cannot be widely dispersed. An inversion of several days can cause an air pollution episode.

IONIZATION CHAMBER - A device roughly similar to a geiger counter that reveals the presence of ionizing radiation.

ISOTOPE - A variation of an element having the same atomic number as the element itself, but having a different atomic weight because of a different number of neutrons. Different isotopes of the same element have different radioactive behavior.

L

LAGOON - In waste water treatment, a shallow pond usually man-made where sunlight, bacterial action, and oxygen interact to restore waste water to a reasonable state of purity.

LATERAL SEWERS - Pipes running underneath city streets that collect sewage from homes or businesses.

LC_{50} - Median lethal concentration, a standard measure of toxicity.

LC_{50} indicates the concentration of a substance that will kill 50 percent of a group of experimental insects or animals.

LEACHATE - Liquid that has percolated through solid waste or other mediums and has extracted dissolved or suspended materials from it.

LEACHING - The process by which soluble materials in the soil, such as nutrients, pesticide chemicals or contaminants, are washed into a lower layer of soil or are dissolved and carried away by water.

LEAD - A heavy metal that may be hazardous to human health if breathed or ingested.

LIFE CYCLE - The phases, changes or stages an organism passes through during its lifetime.

LIFT - In a sanitary landfill, a compacted layer of solid waste and the top layer of cover material.

LIMNOLOGY - The study of the physical, chemical, meteorological, and biological aspects of fresh waters.

M

MARSH - A low-lying tract of soft, wet land that provides an important ecosystem for a variety of plant and animal life but often is destroyed by dredging and filling.

MASKING - Covering over of one sound or element by another. Quantitatively, masking is the amount of audibility threshold of one sound is raised by the presence of a second masking sound. Also used in regard to odors.

MECHANICAL TURBULENCE - The erratic movement of air caused by local obstructions, such as buildings.

MERCURY - A heavy metal, highly toxic if breathed or ingested. Mercury is residual in the environment, showing biological accumulation in all aquatic organisms, especially fish and shellfish. Chronic exposure to airborne mercury can have serious effect on the central nervous system.

METHANE - Colorless, nonpoisonous, and flammable gaseous hydrocarbon. Methane (CA) is emitted by marshes and by dumps undergoing anaerobic decomposition.

MOD - Millions of gallons per day. Mgd is commonly used to express rate of flow.

MICROBES - Minute plant or animal life. Some disease-causing microbes exist in sewage.

MIST - Liquid particles in air formed by condensation of vaporized liquids. Mist particles vary from 500 to 40 microns in size. By comparison, fog particles are smaller than 40 microns in size. MIXED LIQUOR - A mixture of activated sludge and water containing organic matter undergoing activated sludge treatment in the aeration tank.

MOBILE SOURCE - A moving source of air pollution such as an automobile.

MONITORING - Periodic or continuous determination of the amount of pollutants or radioactive contamination present in the environment.

MUCK SOILS - Soils made from decaying plant materials.

MULCH - A layer of wood chips, dry leaves, straw, hay, plastic strips or other material placed on the soil around plants to retain moisture, to prevent weeds from growing, and to enrich soil.

N

NATURAL GAS - A fuel gas occurring naturally in certain geologic formation. Natural gas is usually a combustible mixture of methane and hydrocarbons.

NATURAL SELECTION - The natural process by which the organisms best adapted to their environment survive and those less well adapted are eliminated.

NECROSIS - Death of plant cells resulting in a discolored, sunken area or death of the entire plant.

NITRIC OXIDE (NO) - A gas formed in great part from atmospheric nitrogen and oxygen when combustion takes place under high temperature and high pressure, as in internal combustion engines. NO is not itself a pollutant; however, in the ambient air, it converts to nitrogen dioxide, a major contributor to photochemical smog.

NITROGEN DIOXIDE (NO_2) - A compound produced by the oxidation of nitric oxide in the atmosphere; a major contributor to photochemical smog.

NITROGENOUS WASTES - Wastes of animal or plant origin that contain a significant concentration of nitrogen.

NO - A notation meaning oxides of nitrogen. (See NITRIC OXIDE)

NOISE - Any undesired audible signal. Thus, in acoustics, noise is any undesired sound.

NTA - Nitrilotriacetic acid, a compound once used to replace phosphates in detergents.

NUCLEAR POWER PLANT - Any device, machine, or assembly that converts nuclear energy into some form of useful power, such as mechanical or electrical power. In a nuclear electric power plant, heat produced by a reactor is generally used to make steam to drive a turbine that in turn drives an electric generator.

NUTRIENTS - Elements or compounds essential as raw materials for organism growth and development; for example, carbon, oxygen, nitrogen, and phosphorus.

<u>O</u>

OIL SPILL - The accidental discharge of oil into oceans, bays or inland waterways. Methods of oil spill control include chemical dispersion, combustion, mechanical containment, and absorption.

OLIGOTROPHIC LAKES - Deep lakes that have a low supply of nutrients and thus contain little organic matter. Such lakes are characterized by high water transparency and high dissolved oxygen. OPACITY - Degree of obscuration of light. For example, a window has zero opacity; a wall is 100 percent opaque. The Ringelmann system of evaluating smoke density is based on opacity. OPEN BURNING - Uncontrolled burning of wastes in an open dump.

OPEN DUMP - (See DUMP)

ORGANIC - Referring to or derived from living organisms. In chemistry, any compound containing carbon.

ORGANISM - Any living human, plant or animal.

ORGANOPHOSPHATES - A group of pesticide chemicals containing phosphorus, such as malathion and parathion, intended to control insects. These compounds are short-lived and, therefore, do not normally contaminate the environment. However, some organophosphates, such as parathion, are extremely toxic when initially applied and exposure to them can interfere with the normal processes of the nervous system, causing convulsions and eventually death. Malathion, on the other hand, is low in toxicity and relatively safe for humans and animals. It is a common ingredient in household insecticide products.

OUTFALL - The mouth of a sewer, drain or conduit where an effluent is discharged into the receiving waters.

OVERFIRE AIR - Air forced into the top of an incinerator to fan the flame.

OXIDANT - Any oxygen containing substance that reacts chemically in the air to produce new substances. Oxidants are the primary contributors to photochemical smog.

OXIDATION - A chemical reaction in which oxygen unites or combines with other elements. Organic matter is oxidized by the action of aerobic bacteria; thus, oxidation is used in waste water treatment to break down organic wastes.

OXIDATION POND - A man-made lake or pond in which organic wastes are reduced by bacterial action. Often oxygen is bubbled through the pond to speed the process.

OZONE (O_2) - A pungent, colorless, toxic gas. Ozone is one component of photochemical smog and is considered a major air pollutant.

<u>P</u>

PACKAGE PLANT - A prefabricated or prebuilt waste water treatment plant.

PACKED TOWER - An air pollution control device in which polluted air is forced upward through a tower packed with crushed rock or wood chips while the liquid is sprayed downward on the packing material. The pollutants in the air stream either dissolve or chemically react with the liquid.

PAN - Peroxyacetyl nitrate, a pollutant created by the action of sunlight on hydrocarbons and nitrogen oxides in the air. PANS are an integral part of photochemical smog.

PARTICULATES - Finely divided solid or liquid particles in the air or in air emission. Particulates include dust, smoke, fumes, mist, spray, and fog.

PARTICULATE LOADING - The introduction of particulates into the ambient air.

PATHOGENIC - Causing or capable of causing disease.

PCBs - Polychlorinated biphenyls, a group of organic compounds used in the manufacture of plastics. In the environment, PCBs exhibit many of the same characteristics as DDT and may, therefore, be confused with that pesticide. PCBs are highly toxic to aquatic life; they persist in the environment for long periods of time, and they are biologically accumulative.

PEAT - Partially decomposed organic material.

PERCOLATION - Downward flow or infiltration of water through the pores or spaces of a rock or soil.

PERSISTENT PESTICIDES - Pesticides that will be present in the environment for longer than one growing season or one year after application.

PESTICIDE - An agent used to control pests. This includes insecticides for use against harmful insects, herbicides for weed control, fungicides for control of plant diseases, rodenticides for killing rats, mice, etc., and germicides used in disinfectant products, algaecides, slimicides, etc. Some pesticides can contaminate water, air or soil and accumulate in man, animals, and the environment, particularly if they are misused. Certain of these chemicals have been shown to interfere with the reproductive processes of predatory birds and possibly other animals.

PESTICIDE TOLERANCE - A scientifically and legally established limit for the amount of chemical residue that can be permitted to remain in or on a harvested food or feed crop as a result of the application of a chemical for pest-control purposes. Such tolerances or safety levels, established federally by EPA, are set well below the point at which residues might be harmful to consumers.

pH - A measure of the acidity or alkalinity of a material, liquid, or solid. pH is represented on a scale of 0 to 14, with 7 representing a neutral state, 0 representing the most acid and 14, the most alkaline.

PHENOLS - A group of organic compounds that in very low concentrations produce a taste and odor problem in water. In higher concentrations, they are toxic to aquatic life. Phenols are byproducts of petroleum refining, tanning and textile, dye and resin manufacture.

PHOSPHORUS - An element that, while essential to life, contributes to the eutrophication of lakes and other bodies of water.

PHOTOCHEMICAL OXIDANTS - Secondary pollutants formed by the action of nitrogen and hydrocarbons in the air; they are the primary contributors to photochemical smog.

PHOTOCHEMICAL SMOG - Air pollution associated with oxidants rather than with sulfur oxides, particulates, etc. Produces necrosis, chlorosis, and growth alterations in plants and is an eye and respiratory irritant in humans.

PHYTOPLANKTON - The plant portion of plankton.

PHYTOTOXIC - Injurious to plants.

PIG - A container usually made of lead used to ship or store radioactive materials.

PILE - A nuclear reactor.

PLANKTON - The floating or weakly swimming plant and animal life in a body of water, often microscopic in size.

PLUME - The visible emission from a flue or chimney.

POINT SOURCE - In air pollution, a stationary source of a large individual emission, generally of an industrial nature. This is a general definition; point source is legally and precisely defined in Federal regulations. (See AREA SOURCE)

POLLEN - A fine dust produced by plants; a natural or background air pollutant.

POLLUTANT - Any introduced gas, liquid or solid that makes a resource unfit for a specific purpose.

POLLUTION - The presence of matter or energy whose nature, location, or quantity produces undesired environmental effects.

POLYELECTROLYTES - Synthetic chemicals used to speed flocculation of solids in sewage.

POTABLE WATER - Water suitable for drinking or cooking purposes from both health and aesthetic considerations.

PPM - Parts per million. The unit commonly used to represent the degree of pollutant concentration where the concentrations are small. Larger concentrations are given in percentages. Thus, BOD is represented in ppm, while suspended solids in water are expressed in percentages. In air, ppm is usually a volume/volume ratio; in water, a weight/volume ratio.

PRECIPITATE - A solid that separates from a solution because of some chemical or physical change or the formation of such a solid.

PRECIPITATORS - In pollution control work, any of a number of air pollution control devices usually using mechanical/electrical means to collect particulates from an emission.

PRETREATMENT - In waste water treatment, any process used to reduce pollution load before the waste water is introduced into a main sewer system or delivered to a treatment plant for substantial reduction of the pollution load.

PRIMARY TREATMENT - The first stage in waste water treatment in which substantially all floating or settleable solids are mechanically removed by screening and sedimentation.

PROCESS WEIGHT - The total weight of all materials, including fuels, introduced into a manufacturing process. The process weight is used to calculate the allowable rate of emission of pollutant matter from the process.

PULVERIZATION - The crushing or grinding of material into small pieces.

PUMPING STATION - A station at which sewage is pumped to a higher level. In most sewer systems, pumping is unnecessary; waste water flows by gravity to the treatment plant.

PUTRESCIBLE - Capable of being decomposed by microorganisms with sufficient rapidity to cause nuisances from odors, gases, etc. For example, kitchen wastes or dead animals.

Q

QUENCH TANK - A water-filled tank used to cool incinerator residues.

R

RAD - A unit of measurement of any kind of radiation absorbed by man.

RADIATION - The emission of fast atomic particles or rays by the nucleus of an atom. Some elements are naturally radioactive while others become radioactive after bombardment with neutrons or other particles. The three major forms of radiation are alpha, beta, and gamma.

RADIATION STANDARDS - Regulations that include exposure standards, permissible concentrations and regulations for transportation.

RADIOBIOLOGY - The study of the principles, mechanisms, and effects of radiation on living matter.

RADIOECOLOGY - The study of the effects of radiation on species of plants and animals in natural communities.

RADIOISOTOPES - Radioactive isotopes. Radioisotopes, such as cobalt-60, are used in the treatment of disease.

RASP - A device used to grate solid waste into a more manageable material, ridding it of much of its odor.

RAW SEWAGE - Untreated domestic or commercial waste water.

RECEIVING WATERS - Rivers, lakes, oceans, or other bodies that receive treated or untreated waste waters.

RECYCLING - The process by which waste materials are transformed into new products in such a manner that the original products may lose their identity.

RED TIDE - A proliferation or bloom of a certain type of plankton with red-to-orange coloration, that often causes massive fish kills. Though they are a natural phenomenon, blooms are believed to be stimulated by phosphorus and other nutrients discharged into waterways by man.

REFUSE - (See SOLID WASTE)

REFUSE RECLAMATION - The process of converting solid waste to saleable products. For example, the composting of organic solid waste yields a saleable soil conditioner.

REM - A measurement of radiation dose to the internal tissues of man.

REP - A unit of measurement of any kind of radiation absorbed by man.

RESERVOIR - A pond, lake, tank, or basin, natural or man-made, used for the storage, regulation, and control of water.

RESOURCE RECOVERY - The process of obtaining materials or energy, particularly from solid waste.

REVERBERATION - The persistence of sound in an enclosed space after the sound source has stopped.

RINGELMANN CHART - A series of illustrations ranging from light grey to black used to measure the opacity of smoke emitted from stacks and other sources. The shades of grey simulate various moke densities and are assigned numbers ranging from one to five. Ringelmann No. 1 is equivalent to 20 percent dense; No. 5 is 100 percent dense. Ringelmann charts are used in the setting and enforcement of emission standards.

RIPARIAN RIGHTS - Rights of a land owner to the water on or bordering his property, including the right to prevent diversion or misuse of upstream water.

RIVER BASIN - The total area drained by a river and its tributaries.

RODENTICIDE - A chemical or agent used to destroy or prevent damage by rats or other rodent pests. (See PESTICIDE)

ROUGH FISH - Those fish species considered to be of poor fighting quality when taken on tackle or of poor eating quality; for example, gar, suckers, etc. Most rough fish are more tolerant of widely changing environmental conditions than are game fish.

RUBBISH - A general term for solid waste, excluding food waste and ashes, taken from residences, commercial establishments, and institutions.

RUNOFF - The portion of rainfall, melted snow, or irrigation water that flows across ground surface and eventually is returned to streams. Runoff can pick up pollutants from the air or the land and carry them to the receiving waters.

S

SALINITY - The degree of salt in water.

SALT WATER INTRUSION - The invasion of salt water into a body of fresh water, occurring in either surface or groundwater bodies. When this invasion is caused by oceanic waters, it is called sea water intrusion.

SALVAGE - The utilization of waste materials.

SANITATION - The control of all the factors in man's physical environment that exercise or can exercise a deleterious effect on his physical development, health, and survival.

SANITARY LANDFILL - A site for solid waste disposal using sanitary landfilling techniques.

SANITARY LANDFILLING - An engineered method of solid waste disposal on land in a manner that protects the environment; waste is spread in thin layers, compacted to the smallest practical volume and covered with soil at the end of each working day. SANITARY SEWERS - Sewers that carry only domestic or commercial sewage. Storm water runoff is carried in a separate system. (See SEWER)

SCRAP - Discarded or rejected materials that result from manufacturing or fabricating operations and are suitable for reprocessing.

SCREENING - The removal of relatively coarse floating and suspended solids by straining through racks or screens.

SCRUBBER - An air pollution control device that uses a liquid spray to remove pollutants from a gas stream by absorption or chemical reaction. Scrubbers also reduce the temperature of the emission.

SECONDARY TREATMENT - Waste water treatment, beyond the primary stage, in which bacteria consume the organic parts of the wastes. This biochemical action is accomplished by use of trickling filters or the activated sludge process. Effective secondary treatment removes virtually all floating and settleable solids and approximately 90 percent of both BOD_3 and suspended solids. Customarily, disinfection by chlorination is the final stage of the secondary treatment process.

SEDIMENTATION - In waste water treatment, the settling out of solids by gravity.

SEDIMENTATION TANKS - In waste water treatment, tanks where the solids are allowed to settle or to float as scum. Scum is skimmed off; settled solids are pumped to incinerators, digesters, filters, or other means of disposal.

SEEPAGE - Water that flows through the soil.

SELECTIVE HERBICIDE - A pesticide intended to kill only certain types of plants, especially broad-leafed weeds, and not harm other plants such as farm crops or lawn grasses. The leading herbicide in the United States is 2,4-D. A related but stronger chemical used mostly for brush control on range, pasture, and forest lands and on utility or highway rights-of-way is 2,4,5-T. Uses of the latter chemical have been somewhat restricted because of laboratory evidence that it or a dioxin contaminant in 2,4,5-T can cause birth defects in test animals.

SENESCENCE - The process of growing old. Sometimes used to refer to lakes nearing extinction.

SEPTIC TANK - An underground tank used for the deposition of domestic wastes. Bacteria in the wastes decompose the organic matter, and the sludge settles to the bottom. The effluent flows through drains into the ground. Sludge is pumped out at regular intervals.

SETTLEABLE SOLIDS - Bits of debris and fine matter heavy enough to settle out of waste water.

SETTLING CHAMBER - In air pollution control, a low-cost device used to reduce the velocity of flue gases usually by means of baffles, promoting the settling of fly ash.

SETTLING TANK - In waste water treatment, a tank or basin in which settleable solids are removed by gravity.

SEWAGE - The total of organic waste and waste water generated by residential and commercial establishments.

SEWAGE LAGOON - (See LAGOON)

SEWER - Any pipe or conduit used to collect and carry away sewage or storm water runoff from the generating source to treatment plants or receiving streams. A sewer that conveys household and commercial sewage is called a sanitary sewer. If it transports runoff from rain or snow, it is called a storm sewer. Often storm water runoff and sewage are transported in the same system or combined sewers.

SEWERAGE - The entire system of sewage collection, treatment, and disposal. Also applies to all effluent carried by sewers, whether it is sanitary sewage, industrial wastes, or storm water runoff.

SHIELD - A wall that protects workers from harmful radiation released by radioactive materials.

SILT - Finely divided particles of soil or rock. Often carried in cloudy suspension in water and eventually deposited as sediment.

SINKING - A method of controlling oil spills that employs an agent to entrap oil droplets and sink them to the bottom of the body of water. The oil and sinking agent are eventually biologically degraded.

SKIMMING - The mechanical removal of oil or scum from the surface of water.

SLUDGE - The construction of solids removed from sewage during waste water treatment. Sludge disposal is then handled by incineration, dumping, or burial.

SMOG - Generally used as an equivalent of air pollution, particularly associated with oxidants.

SMOKE - Solid particles generated as a result of the incomplete combustion of materials containing carbon.

SO_x - A symbol meaning oxides of sulfur.

SOFT DETERGENTS - Biodegradable detergents.

SOIL CONDITIONER - A biologically stable organic material such as humus or compost that makes soil more amenable to the passage of water and to the distribution of fertilizing material, providing a better medium for necessary soil bacteria growth.

SOLID WASTE - Useless, unwanted or discarded material with insufficient liquid content to be free flowing. Also see WASTE. (1)

   (1) Agricultural - solid waste that results from the raising and slaughtering of animals, and the processing of animal products and orchard and field crops.

   (2) Commercial - waste generated by stores, offices, and other activities that do not actually turn out a product.

   (3) Industrial - waste that results from industrial processes and manufacturing.

   (4) Institutional - waste originating from educational, health care, and research facilities.

   (5) Municipal - residential and commercial solid waste generated within a community.

   (6) Pesticide - the residue from the manufacturing, handling or use of chemicals intended for killing plant and animal pests.

   (7) Residential - waste that normally originates in a residential environment. Sometimes called domestic solid waste.

SOLID WASTE DISPOSAL - The ultimate disposition of refuse that cannot be salvaged or recycled.

SOLID WASTE MANAGEMENT - The purposeful, systematic control of the generation, storage, collection, transport, separation, processing, recycling, recovery, and disposal of solid wastes.

SONIC BOOM - The tremendous booming sound produced as a vehicle, usually a supersonic jet airplane, exceeds the speed of sound, and the shock wave reaches the ground.

SOOT - Agglomerations of tar-impregnated carbon particles that form when carbonaceous material does not undergo complete combustion.

SORPTION - A term including both adsorption and absorption. Sorption is basic to many processes used to remove gaseous and particulate pollutants from an emission and to clean up oil spills.

SPOIL - Dirt or rock that has been removed from its original location, specifically materials that have been dredged from the bottom of waterways.

STABILIZATION - The process of converting active organic matter in sewage sludge or solid wastes into inert, harmless material.

STABILIZATION PONDS - (See LAGOON, OXIDATION POND)

STABLE AIR - An air mass that remains in the same position rather than moving in its normal horizontal and vertical directions. Stable air does not disperse pollutants and can lead to high build-ups of air pollution.

STACK - A smokestack; a vertical pipe or flue designed to exhaust gases and suspended particulate matter.

STACK EFFECT - The upward movement of hot gases in a stack due to the temperature difference between the gases and the atmosphere.

STAGNATION - Lack of wind in an air mass or lack of motion in water. Both cases tend to entrap and concentrate pollutants.

STATIONARY SOURCE - A pollution emitter that is fixed rather than moving as an automobile.

STORM SEWER - A conduit that collects and transports rain and snow runoff back to the ground water. In a separate sewerage system, storm sewers are entirely separate from those carrying domestic and commercial waste water.

STRATIFICATION - Separating into layers.

STRIP MINING - A process in which rock and top soil strat overlying ore or fuel deposits are scraped away by mechanical shovels. Also known as surface mining.

SULFUR DIOXIDE
(SO_2) - A heavy, pungent, colorless gas formed primarily by the combustion of fossil fuels. SO_2 damages the respiratory tract as well as vegetation and materials and is considered a major air pollutant.

SUMP - A depression or tank that serves as a drain or receptacle for liquids for salvage or disposal.

SURFACTANT - An agent used in detergents to cause lathering. Composed of several phosphate compounds, surfactants are a source of external enrichment thought to speed the eutrophication of our lakes.

SURVEILLANCE SYSTEM - A monitoring system to determine environmental quality. Surveillance systems should be established to monitor all aspects of progress toward attainment of environmental standards and to identify potential episodes of high pollutant concentrations in time to take preventive action.

SUSPENDED SOLIDS (SS) - Small particles of solid pollutants in sewage that contribute to turbidity and that resist separation by conventional means. The examination of suspended solids and the BOD test constitute the two main determinations for water quality performed at waste water treatment facilities.

SYNERGISM - The cooperative action of separate substances so that the total effect is greater than the sum of the effects of the substances acting independently.

SYSTEMIC PESTICIDE - A pesticide chemical that is carried to other parts of a plant or animal after it is injected or taken up from the soil or body surface.

T

TAILINGS - Second grade or waste material derived when raw material is screened or processed.

TERTIARY TREATMENT - Waste water treatment beyond the secondary or biological stage that includes removal of nutrients such as phosphorus and nitrogen and a high percentage of suspended solids. Tertiary treatment, also known as advanced waste treatment, produces a high quality effluent.

THERMAL POLLUTION - Degradation of water quality by the introduction of the heated effluent. Primarily a result of the discharge of cooling waters from industrial processes, particularly from electrical power generation. Even small deviations from normal water temperatures can affect aquatic life. Thermal pollution usually can be controlled by cooling towers.

THRESHOLD DOSE - The minimum dose of given substance necessary to produce a measurable physiological or psychological effect.

TOLERANCE - The relative capability of an organism to endure an unfavorable environmental factor. The amount of a chemical considered safe on any food to be eaten by man or animals. (See PESTICIDE TOLERANCE)

TOPOGRAPHY - The configuration of a surface area including its relief or relative elevations and the position of its natural and man-made features.

TOXICANT - A substance that kills or injures an organism through its chemical or physical action or by altering its environment; for example, cyanides, phenols, pesticides or heavy metals. Especially used for insect control.

TOXICITY - The quality or degree of being poisonous or harmful to plant or animal life.

TRICKLING FILTER - A device for the biological or secondary treatment of waste water consisting of a bed of rocks or stones that support bacterial growth. Sewage is trickled over the bed, enabling the bacteria to break down organic wastes.

TROPOSPHERE - The layer of the atmosphere extending seven to ten miles above the earth. Vital to life on earth, it contains clouds and moisture that reach earth as rain or snow.

TURBIDIMETER - A device used to measure the amount of suspended solids in a liquid.

TURBIDITY - A thick, hazy condition of air due to the presence of particulates or other pollutants, or the similar cloudy condition in water due to the suspension of silt or finely divided organic matter.

U

URBAN RUNOFF - Storm water from city streets and gutters that usually contains a great deal of litter and organic and bacterial wastes.

V

VAPOR - The gaseous phase of substances that normally are either liquids or solids at atmospheric temperature and pressure; for example, steam and phenolic compounds.

VAPOR PLUME - The stack effluent consisting of flue gas made visible by condensed water droplets or mist.

VAPORIZATION - The change of a substance from the liquid to the gaseous state. One of three basic contributing factors to air pollution; the others are attrition and combustion.

VARIANCE - Sanction granted by a governing body for delay or exception in the application of a given law, ordinance, or regulation.

VECTOR - Disease vector - a carrier, usually an arthropod, that is capable of transmitting a pathogen from one organism to another.

VOLATILE -Evaporating readily at a relatively low temperature.

W

WASTE - Also see SOLID WASTE.

(1) Bulky waste - items whose large size precludes or complicates their handling by normal collection, processing, or disposal methods.

(2) Construction and demolition waste - building materials and rubble resulting from construction, remodeling, repair, and demolition operations.

(3) Hazardous waste - wastes that require special handling to avoid illness or injury to persons or damage to property.

(4) Special waste - those wastes that require extraordinary management.

(5) Wood pulp waste - wood or paper fiber residue resulting from a manufacturing process.

(6) Yard waste - plant clippings, prunings, and other discarded material from yards and gardens. Also known as yard rubbish.

WASTE WATER - Water carrying wastes from homes, businesses, and industries that is a mixture of water and dissolved or suspended solids.

WATER POLLUTION - The addition of sewage, industrial wastes, or other harmful or objectionable material to water in concentrations or in sufficient quantities to result in measurable degradation of water quality.

WATER QUALITY CRITERIA - The levels of pollutants that affect the suitability of water for a given use. Generally, water use classification includes: public water supply, recreation, propagation of fish and other aquatic life, agricultural use and industrial use.

WATER QUALITY STANDARD - A plan for water quality management containing four major elements: the use (recreation, drinking water, fish and wildlife propagation, industrial, or agricultural) to be made of the water; criteria to protect those uses; implementation plans (for needed industrial-municipal waste treatment improvements); and enforcement plans, and on anti-degration statement to protect existing high quality waters.

WATERSHED - The area drained by a given stream.

WATER SUPPLY SYSTEM - The system for the collection, treatment, storage, and distribution of potable water from the sources of supply to the consumer.

WATER TABLE - The upper level of ground water.

Z

ZOOPLANKTON - Planktonic animals that supply food for fish.

CPSIA information can be obtained
at www.ICGtesting.com
Printed in the USA
BVHW011430171219
566926BV00012B/412/P